Anxiously Yours

MADHURA VAYAL

notionpress.com

INDIA · SINGAPORE · MALAYSIA

ISBN
Paperback 979-8-89777-959-8
Hardcase 979-8-89906-281-0

About the Author

Madhura Vayal's journey is one of resilience, transformation, and an unshakable commitment to health and healing. Born on September 4, 1981, to a doctor mother and a banker father, Madhura grew up as the younger sister to an accomplished engineer. She often felt like the "ugly duckling" in a family of high achievers, struggling to find her own path. Little did she know that her challenges—both personal and health-related—would one day shape her into a guiding force in the world of nutrition and wellness.

Academically inclined yet deeply passionate about food and its impact on health, Madhura pursued a **B.Sc. in Food Nutrition and Dietetics from Mumbai University**, followed by a **postgraduate diploma in the same field from SNDT Women's University, Pune**. Her thirst for knowledge took her to the **University of Kentucky, U.S., where she completed an M.S. in Nutritional Sciences**. She further expanded her expertise with a **certificate in Plant-Based Nutrition from eCornell** and became a **certified NLP consultant**, adding a psychological and behavioural dimension to her approach to healing.

However, it wasn't just academics that shaped Madhura's perspective—it was her own struggles with health. At 17, she underwent an emergency **appendix removal**, marking the beginning of a long battle with health complications. She was diagnosed with **PCOD**, which brought hormonal imbalances, weight fluctuations, and a myriad of related issues. The mental toll of these struggles led to **severe anxiety and depression**, making even the simplest aspects of life feel overwhelming.

Just when she thought she was finding stability, life threw another challenge her way—**a stroke that left her partially paralysed**. The recovery was long, painful, and filled with uncertainty, but Madhura refused to give up. Even after regaining mobility, her health battles weren't over. A sudden and **emergency gallbladder removal** forced her and her husband, Rajesh Vayal, to re-evaluate everything about their lifestyle. Determined to break the cycle of illness, Rajesh dove deep into research, and together they embraced a **whole-food, plant-based lifestyle**—a decision that changed everything.

Fueled by her personal transformation, Madhura returned to India and joined **SHARAN India** as a consultant and facilitator. Over the past **12 years**, she has touched thousands of lives through **detox programs, affirmations and gratitude workshops, fruit challenges, one-on-one consultations**, and as a **facilitator at SHARAN's prestigious 21-day disease reversal residency program**. Her mission has always been clear: to empower people to take charge of their health and heal naturally.

In **January 2020**, she took her passion a step further and founded **The Gratitude Kitchen**, a plant-based cloud kitchen dedicated to serving **wholesome, nourishing meals free from processed ingredients**. In just five years, the kitchen has served over **60,000 meals**, proving that healthy food can be delicious, accessible, and transformative.

Beyond her professional achievements, Madhura finds her greatest joy in her family. She is married to **Rajesh Vayal**, the driving force behind their shift to plant-based living, and together they have two beautiful children who follow the same lifestyle, thriving in health and abundance.

Madhura's journey—from struggling with chronic illnesses to becoming a leading voice in the plant-based movement—is a testament to the power of resilience, education, and the willingness to embrace change. Through her work, she continues to inspire countless others to take control of their health and discover the healing power of food.

Acknowledgements

As I sit down to write these words of gratitude, my heart is filled with immense appreciation for the people who have been an integral part of my journey—both in life and in the making of this book. *Anxiously Yours* *is* a reflection of my struggles, my victories, and the lessons I have learned along the way. And none of it would have been possible without the unwavering support, love, and guidance of those who stood by me in my darkest moments and celebrated with me in my triumphs.

My Heart, My Home — Rajesh, Reva, and Ram

To **Rajesh, my rock, my friend, and my greatest pillar of strength**—you have been my anchor through the roughest storms. From the moment you stepped into my life, you have believed in me even when I couldn't believe in myself. It was you who led us down the path of whole-food, plant-based living, transforming not just our health but our entire perspective on life. When my health was at its worst, when I struggled to even recognize myself, you stood by me, researching, learning, and guiding me toward a better future. You have never once let me feel alone in my struggles till now, and for that, I am forever grateful.

To my two beautiful children, **Reva and Ram**—you are my greatest blessings. Watching you grow into compassionate, mindful, and health-conscious individuals fills me with immense pride. Your ability to embrace this lifestyle, make conscious choices, and lead with kindness is truly inspiring. You may not fully realize it, but your love, laughter, and innocence have healed me in ways I never thought possible. Every challenge I have faced has been worth it just to see you both thrive. Thank you for being my biggest motivation to keep pushing forward.

My Extended Family — The Roots That Hold Me Steady

To my **mom and sister**, you have been my constant support system from the very beginning. Mom, your dedication as a doctor, your resilience, and your ability to care for others have always inspired me. You taught me the importance of health, though I took a while to fully understand it. To **Yash** and **Sameer**, I know I have always looked up to you in ways I may not have expressed enough. Your achievements, your strength, and your guidance have meant more to me than words can say.

To **Mummy and Papa**, my second set of parents, your love and encouragement have been invaluable. You welcomed me with open arms and have always supported my dreams. Your unwavering faith in me has given me the courage to keep going even when times were tough.

To **Ashley**, Thank you for being there in my tough moments, for listening to me when I needed to let it all out, and for standing by me through my breakdowns. Your kindness and calmness have helped me more than you know. I'm really grateful for you and **Haresh**- Thank you for being my quiet support. Even with your many wise words, you've always been there, and that means so much to me. I'm lucky to have you in my life.

Dr. Nandita Shah — A Beacon of Hope

To **Dr. Nandita Shah**, the founder of **SHARAN India**, I owe so much of my journey in plant-based nutrition to you. Your work in disease reversal has changed countless lives, including mine. Through SHARAN, I found not just a career but a calling. Thank you for your guidance, your wisdom, and your belief in the power of food as medicine. You have been a true inspiration, and I am honored to have had the opportunity to learn from you.

Reyna Rupani — Compassion and Kindness in Action

To **Reyna Rupani**, the CEO of SHARAN India, you have been a guiding force, not just in my professional life but in my personal journey as well. Your compassion, your kindness, and your unwavering belief in the power of awareness have taught me so much. You have shown me that all we need to do is **sow the seed of awareness**, and that is enough to spark transformation. Your love for both humans and animals is truly admirable, and I am so grateful to have had the chance to learn from you.

Dr. Manjeet Prabhugaonkar, Dr Prachi Tripathi and Dr Sujay Prabhugaonkar — Redefining My Relationship with Anxiety

To **Dr. Manjeet, Dr Prachi** and **Dr Sujay** thank you for showing me that anxiety is **not something to be feared**. You helped me see that while it may never completely disappear, it can be **managed beautifully,** allowing me to lead a full and normal life. You gave me the tools to navigate my thoughts, to handle my emotions, and to stop seeing anxiety as a life sentence. Your wisdom and your support have been life-changing, and I will forever be grateful for your guidance.

My Inner Circle — The Ones Who Have Seen It All

To my **dearest friends and family—Shraddha, Kripa, Amol, Rijuta, Santoshi, Smita, Bijal, Vandana, Kommal, Divine Rose, and Archana Gade**—what would I have done without you? You are the ones who have witnessed my highest highs and my lowest lows. You have been there for my rants, my meltdowns, my victories, and my setbacks. No matter what time of day (or night), you have been just a phone call or a WhatsApp message away. Your love, your patience, and your unwavering support have kept me grounded. Thank you for holding space for me, for listening without judgment, and for always reminding me that I am never alone.

To Those Who Came and Went — You Still Matter

There have been many people who have walked into my life at different times, playing an important role in my journey, even if they are no longer present today. Some friendships lasted, some faded, and some ended abruptly. But each one of them contributed in some way to the person I am today. **To every supportive friend who led me to this book, even if we are no longer in each other's lives, I owe you a great deal.** Thank you for the lessons, the memories, and the impact you had on my path.

To My Readers — You Are Not Alone

This book was written for **you**—for every person who has struggled with anxiety, who has felt overwhelmed, who has questioned their strength. If even one sentence in this book brings you comfort, if even one idea helps you navigate a difficult day, then it has served its purpose. I want you to know that **you are not alone** in your journey, and I hope this book feels like a friend to you in times of need.

To My Publishers — For Making This a Reality

Finally, a heartfelt thank you to Rijuta for making my publishing dreams come true- followed by my **publishers Notionpress**, who saw value in this book and believed in its message. Thank you for your patience, your guidance, and for helping shape this book into what it is today. Your willingness to take this project on has given me the opportunity to share my story, and for that, I will always be grateful.

Gratitude Above All

This book would not have been possible without each and every one of you. Your support, your kindness, your belief in me—these are the things that have carried me through. From the bottom of my heart, thank you for being a part of my journey.

With love and gratitude,

– Madhura Vayal

Disclaimer

Dear Reader,

Before you dive into *Anxiously Yours*, I want to take a moment to share something important. This book is not a substitute for professional medical advice, diagnosis, or treatment. It is simply a collection of my personal experiences, reflections, and the coping mechanisms that have helped me navigate the often overwhelming world of anxiety.

Anxiety can manifest in countless ways, and each person's journey is unique. What has worked for me may or may not work for you. This book is not meant to replace therapy, medication, or any other professional help you may need. In my own journey, I have sought therapy, and at times, I have also relied on medication when necessary. Healing is not a one-size-fits-all process—it is deeply personal and often requires a combination of approaches.

That said, I truly believe that the practices, habits, and insights I share in these pages can serve as a starting point, a source of comfort, or even a gentle nudge in the right direction when you find yourself struggling. Some of these tools may help you calm your mind in moments of chaos, while others may bring clarity or a sense of control when everything feels uncertain.

More than anything, my hope is that this book feels like a companion— like a friend sitting beside you, reminding you that you are not alone. Anxiety can be an isolating experience, but I want you to know that there are people who understand, who have been through it, and who are rooting for you. If nothing else, let this book be a reminder that you are seen, you are heard, and you are stronger than you think.

Please take what resonates with you and leave what doesn't. Be kind to yourself as you explore different techniques and strategies. And most importantly, if you are struggling, please reach out for professional help. You deserve support, guidance, and the best possible care on your journey to healing.

If at any point you feel like sharing your thoughts, experiences, or even just saying hello, I would love to hear from you. You can reach me at **madhuravayal2@gmail.com**. Wishing you strength, peace, and moments of joy as you navigate this path.

With love and understanding,

— **Madhura**

How to Use This Book (Without Stressing About It)

Welcome to Anxiously Yours—a book born out of 3 a.m. overthinking, awkward therapy moments, and everyday chaos that somehow always involves missing socks or long alarm snoozes.

This isn't a "10 Steps to Cure Your Anxiety" kind of book—because let's be honest, if that worked, we'd all be calm, glowing unicorns by now. It's a real, raw, and slightly funny account of how anxiety shows up in daily Indian life—and how I've learned to live with it without losing my mind (well, mostly).

Here's how to use it:

1. Read however you like. Front to back, random chapter, or just one page a day. There's no right way. It's your book, your journey.

2. Scribble all over it. Underline lines that hit home. Circle parts that sound exactly like you. Doodle on the margins if that helps. This isn't a textbook—it's a conversation.

3. Try a few tools. At the end of some chapters, you'll find simple techniques I use—journaling prompts, grounding exercises, my MAKERS routine, or even just a comforting thought. Try one or two. No pressure to do it all.

4. Mark your observations. When something clicks—when you suddenly realize "Ohhh, that's why I panic at 4 p.m."—write it down. Capture your "aha" and "uh-oh" moments. Awareness is half the journey.

5. Come back to it. This book isn't a one-time read. Keep it by your bedside, in your bag, or under a pile of laundry you're ignoring. Let it be your gentle reminder that you're not alone.

This isn't about fixing yourself. It's about getting to know yourself with compassion (and maybe a little humor). And every time you see yourself in these pages, know that I wrote this with shaky hands, an open heart, and the hope that it'll make your path feel a little lighter

So, go ahead—read, scribble, underline, breathe, laugh, tr up, and keep going. You've got this. And if not, at least you've got this book.

Contents

About the Author..*3*

Acknowledgements..*7*

Disclaimer..*13*

How to Use This Book (Without Stressing About It)...............*15*

Introduction...*19*

Chapter 1: The Mind of an Anxious Person 29

Chapter 2: Anxiety and the Body 51

Chapter 3: Eating Habits of the Anxious............................73

Chapter 4: Self-Care or Self-Sabotage?...............................94

Chapter 5: The Social Struggle 113

Chapter 6: Developing Coping Mechanisms 125

Chapter 7: Becoming Self-Reliant 146

Chapter 8: Dealing with Setbacks...168

Chapter 9: A Day in the Life of an Anxious (But Surprisingly Capable) Person 185

Chapter 10: Diet Log of an Anxious Person 190

Chapter 11: Thriving, Not Just Surviving...195

Introduction

Why I Want to Write This Book

For as long as I can remember, anxiety has been my constant companion—like that one friend who's both your biggest cheerleader and your worst critic. Let's call it my *frenemy*. Sometimes, it's pushed me to excel, to go the extra mile in academics, extracurriculars, and even in my career. But other times? Oh, it has royally screwed me over—leading to bad relationship decisions, overthinking myself into exhaustion, and turning me into an emotional wreck over things as trivial as an unanswered texts.

Anxiety has been my shadow, my hype-man, my speed bump, and my secret weapon—all rolled into one. And after 43 years of wrestling with it, running from it, resisting it, and then finally *making peace* with it, I've learned one thing: anxiety isn't something to be "fixed" or "cured." It's part of me. And rather than trying to fight it, I've decided to work *with* it. Instead of resisting, I surrender. Instead of treating it like an enemy, I embrace it—sometimes even love it (yes, shocking, I know). It's still an unpredictable rollercoaster, but at least now I've learned how to *buckle up* for the ride.

Has my anxiety been a pain? Absolutely. It has jeopardised relationships (apologies, husband) and made me an over-apologising, overanalysing, over-everything-ing person. But it has also gifted me moments of brilliance—pushing me to take risks I never thought I could, like launching my very own cloud kitchen. It has connected me to incredible mentors (hello, Dr Nandita, Dr. Manjeet, Dr Prachi, Avni) and given me insights about life that I wouldn't trade for anything. It has made me more empathetic, more aware, and—despite all the internal chaos—more *me*.

I'm writing this book for people like me—the over-thinkers, the worriers, the "what-if" dwellers—who feel like their anxiety is running the show. I want you to know that, yes, anxiety is annoying as hell. It will make you second-guess yourself, spiral into imaginary worst-case scenarios, and obsess over things no one else even noticed. But it can *also* be your unexpected superpower.

Behind all the fear, self-doubt, and mental gymnastics, there is *you*—a person who is still capable of doing incredible things, of making a mark, of living a full, meaningful life. You don't have to "fix" yourself to be worthy of happiness, success, or love. You already are.

So, consider this book your friendly (and slightly anxious) companion— here to help you navigate the not-so-good days and appreciate the few *really* good ones. Read on, laugh a little, roll your eyes at how ridiculously relatable this all is, and, most importantly, know that you're not alone.

Now, let's dive in—before I overthink this introduction to death.

Anxiety and Me: A Lifelong Frenemy

Anxiety wasn't always my sidekick. In fact, I was once the kind of toddler who could put even the most fearless daredevils to shame. Picture a tiny, wavy-haired version of me, marching into my first day of school like I owned the place, while other kids clung to their parents and wailed like they were being sent into exile. I strutted in, all smiles, completely unfazed. I didn't cry. Not a single tear. I was a *badass*.

But then, *day three* happened.

By then, I had noticed a trend—every single kid who walked into that classroom was sobbing. Like, full-on hysterics. And I, in my childlike wisdom, figured that *this* was just how school worked. Clearly, the only way to gain entry was to cry your little heart out. So, on the third day, I dramatically burst into tears at the entrance, much to the confusion of my teacher, who had already seen me confidently waltz in on the first two days. My logic? *If I don't cry, they might send me back home. And I like it here!*

See? No anxiety. Just pure, unfiltered childhood logic. I was *that* kid— the one who fought imaginary tigers, engaged in full-contact wrestling matches with my dad, and believed I was invincible. So… where did it all go wrong?

The First Crack

One of my earliest memories of *real* fear—of that chest-tightening, stomach-churning, oh-god-what's-happening feeling—was during an argument between my parents. And when I say *argument*, I don't mean the mild bickering over what's for dinner kind. No, this was a full-blown, escalated fight, complete with smashed plates and a kitchen that looked like a war zone.

And guess who was cleaning it all up?

Yep. *Me and the house helper.*

I must've been around five or six, and I remember my tiny hands picking up broken shards of china, my heart thudding in my chest, trying to process what had just happened. My parents were locked in a bad marriage, at a time when divorce was practically unheard of—taboo, even. My dad, or *Baba*, as I called him, had psychological struggles of his own, but in those days, men seeking mental health help was like asking a fish to climb a tree. It just didn't happen. And my mother, well, she had her own battles to fight.

Now, let me be clear: this isn't about blaming either of them. They were products of their time, doing the best they could with what they had. But for me? That was the moment anxiety made its first grand entrance. And trust me, it didn't leave. It *moved in.*

The Attention-Seeking Rollercoaster

Being the emotional type (*read: a walking sponge for affection*), I craved love, attention, and touch. And when those things weren't available in the way I needed, my subconscious decided, *Fine, we'll get it another way.*

Cue the emotional rollercoaster of *attention-seeking behavior.*

Now, attention-seeking gets a bad rep, but let's be real—when a child isn't getting what they need emotionally, they'll find *creative* ways to fill that gap. Unfortunately, this opened doors to experiences I now wish I could rewrite. It made me an easy target for childhood sexual abuse. It led me into wrong relationships—ones that felt good in the moment but were toxic in the long run. It pushed me straight into the arms of an abusive first marriage, followed by a tumultuous divorce that left me feeling like I had been emotionally run over by a truck.

And then, life decided, *You know what? Let's throw in some physical trauma for fun.*

When Your Body Keeps the Score—Quite Literally

At one point, my body, much like my mind, had just had *enough*. It decided to stage a protest in the form of an overnight stroke, which left me semi-paralyzed. *Because clearly, dealing with anxiety alone wasn't enough—I needed a physical crisis too.*

If you think that was the climax of my personal horror movie, think again. Postpartum depression (PPD) after having my daughter? Check. Emergency gallbladder removal? Check. A lifelong journey of healing while dragging my anxiety along like an annoying yet persistent sidekick? *Triple check.*

Through it all, anxiety never left my side. If anything, it *thrived*. It found new ways to keep me company—through sleepless nights, endless overthinking, and a near-constant inner monologue that sounded like a boardroom full of nervous executives predicting disaster.

But here's the kicker: somewhere along the way, I stopped trying to *fight* it. I stopped seeing it as an enemy and started treating it like that one friend who means well but is just *really bad at calming you down*. Anxiety wasn't going anywhere. So, instead of resisting it, I decided to make it work *for* me.

Did it make me hyper-aware of every possible negative outcome in life? Yes.

Did it also push me to plan, prepare, and work harder than most people? *Also yes.*

Anxiety made me resilient. It made me *aware*. It gave me an edge that I never realized I had. Sure, it still annoys the hell out of me sometimes (*like when I replay a single conversation from three years ago at 2 AM*), but it's also the reason I've made it through *everything*.

And that's why I'm writing this book.

Not to tell you how to "cure" your anxiety (because, honestly, I don't think that's the goal). Not to give you a 10-step guide to inner peace (because, if I had that, trust me, I'd be on a beach sipping coconut water by now). But to remind you that anxiety, despite all its flaws, can *coexist* with success, happiness, and a meaningful life like Marilyn Monroe.

So, if you're reading this and nodding along, thinking, *Wow, this sounds like my life*, then congratulations—you, too, have an anxiety frenemy. Welcome to the club. Let's navigate this mess together.

The Role of Humor in Healing from Anxiety

If you've ever had an anxiety attack in the middle of an otherwise normal day, you know the drill. One minute, you're sipping tea and scrolling through memes, and the next, your brain decides that a slightly delayed text response means the person on the other end *hates you and is plotting your downfall*. Fun, right?

Now, logic would tell you to take a deep breath and *relax*. But anxiety doesn't work like that. Anxiety is like that overenthusiastic coworker who misinterprets every situation and dramatically overreacts:

"Oh, you have a mild headache? Must be a brain tumor."

"You said something slightly awkward? Everyone is talking about it right now."

"You sent a text and didn't get an instant reply? Congratulations, you've lost a friend."

For years, I let this irrational, fear-mongering little voice run the show. But then, something changed. I realized that if I was going to survive this lifelong ride with anxiety, I had two choices: either let it control me or *laugh in its face*. And honestly, the second option sounded way more fun.

Anxiety vs. Badass Toddler Me

There was a time—long before anxiety set up its permanent office in my brain—when I was fearless. I've already told you about my first day of school, where I strutted in like I owned the place while other kids sobbed their way through the gates. But what I didn't tell you? By *day three*, I had *convinced myself* that entering school *required* tears. So, in the most dramatic display of toddler logic, I staged a complete meltdown at the entrance, much to the bewilderment of my teacher, who had literally seen me happily walk in the first two days.

Now, let's pause here. Imagine my teacher's confusion.

Day 1: Confident child.

Day 2: Still chill.

Day 3: *Absolute hysterics.*

This is the exact level of unpredictability that my anxiety operates at. Just when you think I have things figured out, my brain goes, *Nope! Time to panic!*

Anxiety's Favorite Game: Overthink Everything

Fast forward a few decades, and my life now looks like this: I'm an established whole-food plant-based nutritionist, attached to SHARAN, running a vegan cloud kitchen, married to a *health freak* who treats fitness and cricket like a religion, raising two kids, taking care of my in-laws, and dealing with an over independent *doctor mother* and to top it all I have zero work-life balance. If that sentence exhausted you, welcome to my daily life.

And of course, anxiety *loves* chaos. It thrives on it. So while normal people go about their day handling one task at a time, my brain prefers to run multiple catastrophic scenarios at once.

For example, on any given morning, while I'm chopping vegetables for the cloud kitchen, here's what's happening inside my head:

o   *Did I confirm that nutrition workshop for next week?*

o   *What if my daughter's school calls? What if she struggling in her new school?*

o   *Did I put salt in this dish? What if I didn't? Oh my god, I definitely forgot. Nope, I put it in twice. Great, now it's ruined.*

o   *What if my son grows up and decides to hate me for the decisions I took?*

This is why I sometimes put my phone in the fridge and find my car keys in the pantry. Anxiety keeps my brain running on overdrive, and occasionally, things just *short-circuit*.

Anxiety vs. My Fitness-Obsessed Husband

Now, let's talk about my husband. He's into fitness. The kind who *tracks the weights he lifts (he has to be the best lifter in the class), the workouts he does and* his fasting hours like it's a world record attempt. The kind who reminds me that eating at the "wrong time" could mess up my metabolism. (And I am the nutritionist- rolling my eyes while typing this)

And then there's me—eating homemade nutella straight from the jar at *midnight* because anxiety told me to.

Every night, we have some version of this conversation:

Him: "You should really stop eating so late. Your digestion needs rest."

Me: "Oh, I *want* to stop eating late."

Him: "Then just don't eat. Go to sleep"

Me: "Oh, honey, if only I could do that."

Because here's what happens: I lie in bed, ready to sleep, and then my brain whispers, *"Whats the point of counting calories when everything is a mess let's find some comfort in FOOD… right sweetheart?"*

And before I know it, I'm in the kitchen, spooning nutella butter straight into my mouth like a feral animal, telling myself this is healthy justifying what I am doing!!

See, I don't just *go to sleep.* I *prepare* for sleep—by replaying every embarrassing moment of my life since childhood, planning out imaginary arguments for situations that will *never happen,* and overanalyzing a text message I sent seven hours ago. By the time I finally *do* sleep, I've aged two years.

Laughing Through the Madness

At some point, I realized that I had two choices: either let anxiety drive me to exhaustion or *find the humor in it.* So now, when my brain randomly panics about whether I turned the geyser off (*while I'm in the car, miles away from home*), I just roll with it. When I overthink an interaction to the point of absurdity, I narrate it to my husband in an exaggerated, dramatic way—like a one-woman sitcom. And when life throws yet another unexpected challenge my way, I remind myself that I've *literally* survived worse.

Humor is how I take my power back. It's how I remind anxiety that *it doesn't own me.* Sure, it's my lifelong frenemy, but at least now, I get to laugh at its ridiculousness instead of letting it run my life.

So if you're struggling with anxiety, try it. The next time your brain starts spiraling into worst-case scenarios, pause and ask yourself:

o   *Is this really happening, or is this just my anxiety being dramatic again?*

o   *If my friend were saying this, would I laugh at how ridiculous it sounds?*

o   *Can I turn this moment into a funny story later?*

Because sometimes, the best way to heal isn't by fighting anxiety—it's by laughing at it until it gives up and lets you live your life.

Chapter 1

The Mind of an Anxious Person

Overthinking 101: Turning a Simple Text into a Full-Blown Crisis

If overthinking were an Olympic sport, I'd have at least five gold medals by now. It's not just a habit—it's practically my superpower. I can take the simplest situation and turn it into an elaborate thriller with multiple plot twists, emotional breakdowns, and a dramatic (but totally unnecessary) conclusion.

For me, overthinking starts *the moment I open my eyes* and doesn't stop until I finally drift into deep sleep—*if* my brain allows it. It's not just about big things like career decisions or parenting struggles. No, no. My brain believes *everything* is worth a deep-dive analysis.

1. *Why did the grocery delivery guy say "Have a good day" in that tone?*

2. *What if my daughter's teacher secretly thinks I'm a bad mom because I sent her with a slightly messy hair pleat today?*

3. *Did I sound too desperate when I texted "Hey!" with an exclamation mark instead of a full stop?*

4. *Wait, do full stops sound rude now?*

The Text Message Black Hole

If I had to pick the *worst* overthinking trigger, it would be this: sending a message and *not getting a reply.*

It doesn't matter *who* it is—my husband, my best friend, my in-laws, a long-lost cousin, or even *a stranger I met once at a workshop.* If I send a message and see nothing but silence, my brain *spirals into absolute chaos.*

Here's a glimpse into how my thought process works when I send a simple text:

Step 1: The Innocent Beginning

Me: *Hey, how are you?* (Hit send.)

Brain: *Good job! You reached out. Normal human interaction. Nothing to worry about.*

Step 2: The Anxiety Warm-Up (5 minutes in, no reply)

Brain: *Okay, maybe they're busy. No big deal.*

Step 3: The Rapid Decline (30 minutes in, still no reply)

Brain: *Wait, did I say something wrong? Did I use too many emojis? Too few emojis? Did they suddenly start hating me?*

Step 4: The Existential Crisis (1 hour in, still nothing)

Brain: *Oh my god, they're ignoring me. I must have done something terrible. Am I a horrible person?*

Step 5: The Back-Channeling Investigation

At this stage, I start doing *detective work*. I'll check if they've been online, stalk their last seen, re-read our old conversations for clues, and maybe even casually ask a mutual friend if they've heard from them recently—*without looking suspicious, of course.*

Step 6: The Emotional Breakdown

Physical symptoms kick in:

o   Palpitations

o   Sinking feeling in the gut (*as if the world is ending*)

o   Slightly heavy head (*as if I'm carrying the weight of the unsent reply on my shoulders*)

At this point, my husband usually notices something is wrong.

Him: *"Why do you look so stressed?"*

Me: *"Oh, no reason. Just waiting for a text reply."*

Him: *"That's it?"*

Me: *"…You don't understand."*

Finding the Trigger (Because Sometimes, I Don't Even Know)

Here's the thing: sometimes, I don't even *realize* what's triggered my overthinking. I'll just suddenly feel this tight, anxious feeling in my chest, and my brain will go, *"SOMETHING IS WRONG."*

But *what* is wrong? That's the million-dollar question.

So I have to do an internal investigation.

1.   *Is it because of a message?*

2.   *Did someone say something weird to me today?*

3. *Am I feeling guilty about something?*

4. *Did I leave an email unanswered?*

It's like playing detective, except the mystery is inside my own head.

Breaking the Overthinking Cycle

Once I *finally* figure out the trigger, the next step is to tell myself that it's *probably* not as bad as my brain is making it out to be. But let's be honest—rational thinking doesn't always work in the middle of an overthinking episode.

The only thing that truly *ends* the madness is distraction. I have to *physically* do something to stop the endless thought loops.

1. Yoga (*because apparently, deep breathing helps shut up my brain*)

2. Walking (*because moving helps shake off the anxiety*)

3. Journaling (*because dumping all my thoughts on paper makes them look a lot less terrifying*)

4. Cooking (*because chopping vegetables is weirdly therapeutic*)

5. Cleaning (*because at least I get a spotless house out of my overthinking crisis*)

Overthinking: The Ultimate Energy Drain

Here's the worst part about overthinking—it's *exhausting*.

It's like running a mental marathon every single day but *never* reaching the finish line. It drains energy, messes with sleep, and turns small, everyday moments into major emotional events.

But the one thing that helps? *Laughing at it.*

Now, when I catch myself spiraling over a late text reply, I try to take a step back and imagine what I'd say if my friend was doing the same thing.

I'd probably say: *"Chill out! They're probably just busy. It's not that deep."*

So why is it so hard to tell *myself* the same thing?

Because anxiety is sneaky. It makes you believe that *your* overthinking is justified, while everyone else's is silly. But in reality, it's all the same. Just a bunch of unnecessary stress over things that *probably* don't matter.

So, if you're an overthinker like me, here's what I'll tell you:

1. Your brain is *not* a fortune teller.

2. A late reply is *not* the end of the world.

3. You need to be kind to yourself and not beat yourself all the time for other people's actions or for even your reactions.

4. And sometimes, the best way to stop overthinking is to laugh at how ridiculous it all is.

Now, excuse me while I go check my phone again—just *one* more time.

The Art of Catastrophizing: How to Turn a Small Incident into a Full-Blown Disaster

If overthinking is an art, then catastrophizing is *the masterpiece*. It's the grand finale of anxiety, where a minor inconvenience transforms into a *life-altering disaster* within seconds.

I like to think of it as my brain's *favorite pastime*—turning the most ordinary situations into the *worst-case scenario*. And let me tell you, I am a *pro* at this.

Amplified Reactions: A Skill I Never Wanted

Most people react to situations *proportionally*. For example:

1. You text a friend, and they don't reply? *"Oh, they must be busy."*

2. You make a small mistake at work? *"No big deal, I'll fix it."*

3. Your husband is a little quiet today? *"Maybe he's just tired."*

But *my* brain? No, no. It *amplifies* everything. It has one setting: *FULL PANIC MODE.*

Example 1: The Friend Who Didn't Reply

Reality: They're probably just caught up with work, family, or life.

My Brain: *They hate me. They've formed a secret WhatsApp group where they discuss how annoying I am. They are currently planning my social exile.*

Actual Conversation (In My Head):

Me: *"Hey, what's up?"* (Sent at 9:00 AM)

(No reply)

Me: *"Oh no. She must be angry with me."*

(No reply by 12:00 PM)

Me: *"Did I say something wrong? Was it that joke I made last week? Did she take it the wrong way?"*

(No reply by 6:00 PM)

Me: *"That's it. Our friendship is over. I am officially friendless. I will die alone with only my anxiety for company."*

Reality Check (Next Morning):

Friend: *"Hey! Sorry, was super busy with work yesterday. What's up?"*

Me: *"Oh, nothing. Just… you know… EXISTENTIAL CRISIS."*

Example 2: Financial Independence & Ending Up Alone

Reality: I am financially stable and doing well.

My Brain: *But what if something happens? What if I suddenly lose all my money? What if I end up alone with no savings and no one to take care of me?*

Cue dramatic Bollywood scene:

1. Me sitting alone in an empty house with just a dimly lit diya.

2. Flashbacks of all the wrong financial decisions I *might* make in the future.

3. A slow, sad violin playing in the background.

What Actually Happens:

1. I check my accounts. Everything is fine.

2. My husband, *who is very much still here*, is casually drinking smoothie and talking about his intermittent fasting hours.

3. I am not broke. I am not alone. But my brain doesn't care—it loves a good disaster.

Example 3: The Recognition That Never Came

Let's talk about *work*. We all want to be appreciated, right? But for people like me, *not* getting recognition doesn't just feel like a missed opportunity. It feels like *proof* that we are invisible.

Reality: People notice my work, but they don't always say it out loud.

My Brain: *Nobody values me. I am doing all this for NOTHING. I should just disappear and see if anyone even notices!*

Actual Scenario:

Me (after organizing a huge event): *"Wow, that went well!"*

> (Colleague praises someone else for their minor contribution.)

> Me: *"Oh. OH. So I did nothing, huh? It's fine. I'll just sit in a corner and cry."*

> Later, my boss sends a message: *"Great job on the event!"*

> Me: *"…Oh. Maybe I overreacted."*

> (But let's be honest, *it will happen again.*)

Example 4: The Husband Who is *Obviously* Abandoning Me

Reality: We had a *tiny* argument.

My Brain: *THIS IS IT. This is the beginning of the end. He's going to leave me. I will have to explain to the kids why their father has vanished. I will live a lonely life, eating Amma Noodles (healthier version of Maggie) at 2 AM, crying into my non-dairy masala chai.*

Actual Conversation:

> Me: *"You always do this."*

> Him: *"Do what?"*

> Me: *"I don't know, but YOU KNOW."*

> Him: *"Okay, I'm going for my workout."*

Me (thinking): *"He needs space. He's thinking of leaving me. I should prepare for single motherhood."*

(He comes back an hour later, sweaty, smiling, and carrying bananas and fruits for his smoothie.)

> Him: "I got your favorite jackfruit."

Me: "…Okay, maybe you're not abandoning me. But next time, TEXT ME THAT YOU'RE NOT ABANDONING ME."

Example 5: The Never-Enough Syndrome

No matter what I do, there's a voice in my head that says, *"It's not enough."*

1. *Cooked a nice meal?* Could've been better.

2. *Worked hard on a project?* Still not perfect.

3. *Took care of family, work, and everything else?* Others do more.

Indian culture makes this *even worse* because we grow up hearing things like:

1. *"Sharma ji ka beta did this."*

2. *"You should always aim for better."*

3. *"Self-sacrifice is the ultimate virtue."*

So, no matter what I do, I sometimes feel like *I'm failing.*

Solution?

1. Remind myself that *perfection is a myth.*

2. Accept that *Sharma ji's beta is not my competition.*

3. Remember that *doing my best is enough—even if my brain disagrees.*

How to Deal with Catastrophizing (Without Losing Your Mind)

Pause & Reality Check

Before I let my brain jump to *the worst possible scenario*, I take a step back.

1. *Did they REALLY ignore me, or are they just busy?*

2. *Did my husband REALLY mean to hurt me, or was it just a miscommunication?*

Most of the time, the answer is *way less dramatic* than my brain makes it out to be.

Ask Yourself: "What's the Worst That Can Happen?"

When my mind spirals, I try to *logically* answer this question.

1. *If my friend doesn't text back?* I'll live.

2. *If my work isn't recognized?* I'll keep doing what I love.

3. *If my husband and I fight?* We'll make up.

Once I play out *the worst-case scenario*, it doesn't seem that scary anymore.

Find a Distraction

Nothing shuts down a catastrophizing episode like *doing something else*.

1. Yoga (*helps shut my brain up for a while*)

2. Walking (*because movement helps with anxious energy*)

3. Watching trashy reality TV (*because their drama makes mine seem small*)

Laugh at It

Honestly, the best way to deal with catastrophizing is to see how *ridiculous* it is.

1. *A late text does not equal social rejection.*

2. *A minor work setback does not mean career failure.*

3. *One argument does not mean a marriage is over.*

When I catch myself spiraling, I imagine myself as the *dramatic Bollywood heroine*, crying over absolutely nothing. And then I laugh. Because sometimes, *it really is that absurd.*

Final Thoughts: Anxiety Is a Liar, but You Don't Have to Believe It

Catastrophizing makes *every small thing feel like the end of the world.* But the truth is, *most of it is just in our heads.*

So next time my brain tells me that a late reply means I'm being abandoned, or that one mistake means I'm doomed forever—I'll take a deep breath, laugh at my own ridiculousness, and remind myself:

"Not everything is a disaster. Sometimes, it's just a bad WiFi connection."

Decision Paralysis: Why Choosing an Outfit Shouldn't Take an Hour (Or Cause an Existential Crisis)

If there's one thing I have mastered over the years, it's *procrastination through overthinking.* And one of the biggest culprits? *Decision paralysis.*

Now, for those who don't know what that is (*lucky you!*), decision paralysis is when you're faced with a choice—big or small—and instead of making a decision like a normal person, you just... *freeze.* Your brain goes into *analysis mode*, and before you know it, *you've wasted hours, days, or even weeks* on something that should've taken five minutes.

Sounds familiar? *Welcome to my world.*

The Outfit Crisis: A Daily Struggle

Let's start with something seemingly *trivial: choosing an outfit.*

A normal person: *Opens wardrobe, picks an outfit, wears it, and moves on with life.*

Me: *Stares at wardrobe like it holds the secrets of the universe.*

Step 1: The What-If Game

1. *What if I wear this and it suddenly gets too hot?*

2. *What if I wear this and run into someone important?*

3. *What if I wear this and it's a fashion disaster that will haunt me for years?*

Step 2: The Second-Guessing

I pick an outfit, put it on, and then stare at myself in the mirror like a detective analyzing a crime scene.

1. *Is this too much?*

2. *Is this too little?*

3. *Does this make me look like a struggling artist?*

I change. Again. And again. *And again.* Before I know it, *30 minutes have passed,* my bed is covered in rejected outfits, and I'm *still in my towel.*

At this point, my husband—who has been wearing the same three t-shirts in rotation for years—walks in and says, *"Are you still deciding?"*

YES. *YES, I AM.*

Parenting Decisions: The Endless Loop of 'Am I Doing the Right Thing?'

Decision paralysis doesn't just stop at clothes. Oh no. It follows me *everywhere*—especially in *parenting*.

For example, when my kids want to go *anywhere* without me, my brain goes into *full crisis mode*.

Daughter: *"Mumma, can I go to the mall with my friends?"*

Me (internally): *MALL? Alone? Without me? What if she gets lost? What if she meets the wrong crowd?*

Me (out loud): *"…Umm… let me think about it."*

This *thinking* phase? Oh, it can last for *days*.

At night, my brain suddenly whispers: *"What if she gets kidnapped?"* And then I'm on Google, looking up *for incidents at that mall* like a crime investigator.

By the time I finally say *yes*, the event is *already over*, and I have successfully *robbed my child of a social life*.

Work Decisions: The Art of Overanalyzing

Work should be about *efficiency*. But when you suffer from *decision paralysis*, it's anything but.

Example 1: Sending an Important Email

Normal person: *Types email, sends it, done.*

Me:

1. *Writes email.*

2. *Rereads it 50 times.*

3. *Thinks: "Is 'Regards' too formal? Should I say 'Best'? Or should I just say 'Thanks'?"*

4. *Saves email as draft.*

5. *Forgets to send it.*

6. *Panics when the boss asks why I haven't replied.*

Example 2: Scaling My Business

Running a vegan cloud kitchen? Exciting.

Making big business decisions? *Terrifying.*

For months, I debated whether I should expand my menu. Should I offer more dishes? Should I start meal subscriptions? Should I *hire more staff?*

Instead of making a decision, I did what I do best:

1. *Made endless pros-and-cons lists.*

2. *Watched hours of YouTube videos on business growth.*

3. *Asked 10 different people for their opinions.*

And guess what? *I still couldn't decide.*

Until one day, my husband—who operates in a *decide-now-think-later* way—said, *"Just do it. If it works, great. If not, you adjust."*

…Wait, it's that simple?

Relationships & The Fear of Making the Wrong Choice

Decision paralysis isn't just about *small* choices. It also *messes with the big ones*—especially in relationships.

Example 1: The 'Should I Say Something?' Dilemma

A friend hasn't called in a while. Do I text them first? Or will that make me seem *needy*? What if they *don't want* to talk to me?

I overthink, I hesitate, and I do nothing.

Then I sit and sulk that *they didn't reach out either.*

Example 2: The 'One Argument Means Divorce' Panic

My husband and I have a *small* disagreement—maybe over something as stupid as what show to watch.

Does my brain register this as *a minor issue*? Of course not.

My brain: *"This is it. The marriage is crumbling. Soon, we will be discussing custody of the kids."*

Actual conversation:

Me: *"I think we should talk."*

Him: *"About what?"*

Me: *"Our argument."*

Him: *"You mean when I said I prefer cricket over detective web series?"*

Me: *"Yes."*

Him: *"…Okay. Let's talk."*

Five minutes later, we are *laughing about something completely unrelated,* and I realize that my *paralysis* was *pointless.*

Why Does This Happen?

So why do I, and so many others, get stuck in *this cycle of indecision?*

- o **Fear of Making the Wrong Choice**

What if I choose wrong? What if I regret it? What if this one small decision *ruins everything*? (*Spoiler: It won't.*)

o **Perfectionism**

I don't just want to make *a* decision. I want to make the *best* decision. And that search for *perfection* keeps me from making *any* decision.

o **Overloaded Brain = Frozen Brain**

Too many options? *Brain shuts down.*

Breaking Free: How to Stop Overthinking Every Decision

Overcoming decision paralysis isn't *easy*, but I've learned a few tricks that help:

o **The 5-Second Rule**

If a decision isn't *life-altering*, I give myself *5 seconds* to choose. No second-guessing. No debating. *Just decide.*

o **Ask: Will This Matter in a Year?**

Most decisions feel *huge* in the moment. But will it still matter in a *year*? If not, *it's not worth overthinking.*

o **Limit Options**

Too many choices = *brain freeze*. I try to *simplify* my options so I don't get stuck in an endless loop.

o **Accept That No Decision is Perfect**

Sometimes, there *is no* perfect choice. And that's *okay.*

o **Trust Your Gut**

Not *every* decision needs an *Excel sheet*. Sometimes, you just *know.*

Final Thoughts: Done is Better Than Perfect

At the end of the day, *overthinking everything*—from outfits to business decisions—*only wastes time.*

So, next time I'm stuck choosing between two dresses, debating an email, or spiraling over a parenting choice, I'll remind myself:

o   **Not every decision will change my life.**

o   **It's better to choose something than to stay frozen.**

o   **The world won't end if I make the wrong choice.**

And if all else fails, I'll just *flip a coin* and call it a day.

Anxiety vs. Intuition: How to Tell If It's a Gut Feeling or Just Your Overactive Brain Freaking Out

If I got a rupee every time I confused anxiety for intuition, I'd probably be sipping coconut water in Goa instead of sitting here overthinking *this* article.

But let's get real—how often have you felt that *nagging voice* in your head and wondered, *Is this my gut trying to warn me, or am I just being my usual, anxiety-ridden self?*

See, there's a fine line between **intuition** (which is like your wise, all-knowing dadi who somehow just *knows* what's best for you) and **anxiety** (which is like that overprotective aunty who warns you about *everything*, including wearing black (my favourite colour) on Saturdays because "Shani bhagwan will get angry").

So how do you tell the difference? Buckle up, because we're about to break it down—Indian-style.

What is Intuition?

Think of intuition as that calm, inner voice that gently nudges you toward the right decision. It's not loud, it doesn't panic, and it doesn't *yell* at you like your mother when you forget to call her back.

Intuition is:

- **Subtle and calm**

- **Based on deep-rooted wisdom and experience**

- **Feels right, even if it doesn't make logical sense**

Example: You meet someone new, and something *just* feels off. They haven't done anything wrong, but your gut says, *Nope, stay away.* Later, you find out they're the type who borrows money and "forgets" to return it. *That's intuition.*

What is Anxiety?

Anxiety, on the other hand, is that hyperactive monkey in your brain that imagines the **worst possible** scenario for literally everything. It's loud, dramatic, and convinces you that *everything* is a potential disaster.

Anxiety is:

- **Loud and panicky**

- **Comes from fear, not wisdom**

- **Feels overwhelming and urgent**

Example: You send a WhatsApp message. It gets one tick. *One tick!* Immediately, anxiety screams: *They hate you. You must have said something wrong. What if they're ghosting you?* Turns out, their phone was just on airplane mode.

Anxiety vs. Intuition: The Key Differences

Aspect	Intuition	Anxiety
Feeling	Calm, steady	Nervous, frantic
Tone	Gentle, subtle	Loud, urgent
Basis	Deep knowledge, experience	Fear, overthinking
Result	Helps you make better choices	Makes you doubt yourself

Now, let's dive into some **real-life examples** to see how this plays out.

Example 1: The 'Should I Hire This Cook for My Cloud Kitchen?' Dilemma

Running a cloud kitchen is no joke. Between planning menus, handling orders, and making sure your kitchen doesn't look like a war zone, you desperately need a reliable cook. You finally find someone who *seems* perfect—great experience, glowing references, and claims to make the best oil-free curries. But then...

Scenario 1: Intuition Talking

Something feels *off*. Maybe it's the way they avoid eye contact or their overconfident *"Madam, I can handle everything, don't worry"* attitude that reminds you of every overpromising service provider who's let you down.

You listen to your gut and decide to do a trial week first. Sure enough, by Day 3, the person is arriving late, mixing up orders, and has already quit twice before changing their mind. *Good thing you trusted your intuition!*

Scenario 2: Anxiety Talking

Your brain starts spiraling: *What if I don't find anyone else? What if I have to do all the cooking myself? What if this person quits after a month and leaves me in a lurch?*

Now, these aren't actual *red flags*—these are just fears your anxiety is cooking up (pun intended). If there's no logical reason to doubt the person, but you're still freaking out, that's just your overthinking taking the lead.

Example 2: The 'Should I Attend My School Reunion?' Panic

You get a message in the school WhatsApp group: **20-Year Reunion! Let's catch up like old times!**

Your first instinct is excitement—until your brain starts doing its thing.

Scenario 1: Intuition Talking

A quiet voice inside tells you *this might not be the best idea.* Maybe you had a tough time in school, or you know from past meetups that the conversation will revolve around who has the most successful career, the fanciest car, or whose kid got into IIT.

You decide to sit this one out, save yourself the awkwardness, and spend the evening with friends who *actually* make you feel good. No regrets.

Scenario 2: Anxiety Talking

Your brain goes into full drama mode: *What if I don't go and they think I've become a snob? What if everyone has achieved more than me? What if I don't remember anyone's name? What if they only invited me out of courtesy?!*

This is just anxiety overanalyzing a simple social event. If the only reason you're hesitant is because of *what people might think,* then it's probably safe to go. And even if you show up, panic, and leave in 30 minutes, at least you'll know you tried!

Example 3: The Parenting Panic

Your kid wants to go for a school trip. You feel uneasy. But why?

Scenario 1: Intuition Talking

Your gut tells you something is *actually* wrong—maybe you sense that the school's safety measures aren't good enough.

You check, and sure enough, the trip arrangements seem *unorganized.* You decide to skip it. Later, you hear that the bus broke down in the middle of nowhere. *Score one for intuition!*

Scenario 2: Anxiety Talking

Your brain yells: *What if they fall? What if they eat something with dairy unknowingly? What if they forget to call me? What if they get lost?*

If there's no *actual reason* for your worry, it's just your anxiety making you act like an overprotective Bollywood mom.

So, How Do You Tell the Difference?

If you're still confused, here's a quick test:

1. If it feels **like a gentle nudge**, it's probably **intuition.**
2. If it feels **like a screaming banshee**, it's **anxiety.**
3. If it's based on **real past experiences**, it's **intuition.**
4. If it's based on **irrational fear**, it's **anxiety.**

Still unsure? **Wait.** Intuition doesn't rush you. Anxiety makes you feel like you need to decide *right now.*

Final Thoughts: Learning to Trust Yourself

If you're someone who struggles with anxiety (*hi, welcome to the club!*), learning to differentiate between anxiety and intuition takes *time*.

Here's what helps:

o **Breathe & Pause:** If a thought makes you panic, don't act on it immediately.

o **Ask: Is this fear or wisdom?** Fear feels urgent; wisdom feels steady.

o **Check the Evidence:** Is there *real* proof for your worry, or is it just your brain making up stories?

o **Trust Yourself:** The more you listen to your intuition, the stronger it gets.

So, next time your brain starts spinning out of control, take a deep breath and ask yourself: *Is this my gut talking, or is this just my anxiety taking me on another unnecessary roller coaster?*

And if you still can't tell the difference, *just go have chai and think about it later*. Works every time.

Chapter 2

Anxiety and the Body

The Physical Symptoms: Why Does My Stomach Hate Me?

Anxiety is a funny thing. Well, not *funny* funny—more like, "Haha, I ruined my own life again" kind of funny.

One of its most dramatic acts? The absolute **chaos it unleashes on your body**. And at the top of the list is **eating like there's no tomorrow**, even when your brain and stomach both agree that you should probably stop.

But can you? Nope. Because anxiety turns you into a **human vacuum cleaner**, sucking up food with no logic, no reasoning, and absolutely no concern for your digestive system.

It's not even about hunger. You know you're full. Your body knows you're full. Your logical mind is literally *screaming* at you: **"STOP! YOU DON'T NEED THIS!"**

But somehow, your hands are still shoveling food into your mouth.

And then comes the **guilt**—the painful, soul-crushing realization that you just ate yourself into a food coma for no reason. You swear you'll never do it again.

Until the next time.

Welcome to **the anxiety-binge-eating cycle**—an all-you-can-eat buffet of self-sabotage, guilt, and stomachaches.

Let's dig into this (pun intended).

The Many Ways Anxiety Messes with Your Eating Habits

Anxiety doesn't just affect your mind; it has a **VIP pass to your digestive system**. It can make you:

- **Overeat when you're stressed** (because somehow, food feels like a temporary hug)

- **Lose your appetite when you're nervous** (as if your stomach just packed its bags and left)

- **Crave junk food like a possessed demon** (because who craves a salad when they're anxious?)

- **Eat at weird times** (midnight potato chips cravings? Been there.)

But **binge eating due to anxiety** is its own special kind of nightmare.

The Anxiety-Binge-Eating Cycle (Also Known as Self-Sabotage 101)

Step 1: The Emotional Trigger

Maybe it's a fight with your husband. Maybe it's your boss's email saying, *"Let's discuss this later"*. Maybe it's just your brain deciding to overanalyze a random conversation from **2010**.

Boom. **Anxiety activated.**

Step 2: The "I Need Something to Feel Better" Phase

Your body, sensing emotional distress, immediately demands a **distraction**. And what's the easiest, quickest, most satisfying distraction? **FOOD.**

And not just any food—**comfort food.**

Chai and pakoras? Too mild.

Dal chawal? Too healthy.

Five pieces of chocolate, an entire bag of chips, and a family-sized pizza meant for four people? YES.

Step 3: The Mind-Body War Begins

Halfway through eating, your **brain** tries to stage an intervention:

- *You're full. Stop eating.*

- *Eat faster before logic kicks in.*

- *This is self-sabotage.*

- *Shhh. Just enjoy the taste.*

- *You will regret this later.*

- *That's later's problem.*

Step 4: The "Why Am I Like This?" Realization

The food is gone. You're lying on the couch, staring at the ceiling, questioning all your life choices.

Your stomach is **bloated**, your energy levels **crash**, and you feel **like a failure.**

Guilt enters the chat.

And what do you do to deal with this guilt?

You promise yourself: **"Never again."**

Step 5: The Vicious Cycle Continues

Fast forward a few days (or hours). Anxiety strikes again. The cycle repeats itself.

Why? Because anxiety is a **master manipulator**, and food is the quickest way to feel *temporarily* better.

Why Do We Do This? (A.K.A. The Science Behind the Madness)

Turns out, this **isn't just lack of willpower**. It's biology.

1. Anxiety Tricks Your Body Into Thinking It Needs Food

When you're anxious, your body releases **cortisol**, a stress hormone. This **confuses your hunger signals**, making your brain think, *"We need food for survival!"*

But the **stress isn't coming from starvation**, it's coming from your **brain's overactive drama department**.

2. Sugar- Salt-Fat = Instant Mood Lift

Junk food (especially sugar, salt, greasy and carbs) gives you an instant **dopamine hit**—a rush of feel-good chemicals.

For a few moments, everything feels **fine**. Then the crash comes, making you feel worse than before.

3. Habit Formation: Your Brain Loves a Quick Fix

The more you use food to cope with stress, the more your brain starts associating:

Anxiety = Must Eat Something.

Over time, this becomes a **habit**, and habits are **hard to break**.

How Anxiety-Binge Eating Shows Up in Indian Life

1. The "I'll Eat My Feelings" Post-Fight Special

You have a big argument with your husband. He storms off, you fume for 10 minutes, and then **your brain decides food is the answer.**

Cut to: You standing in the kitchen at 11 PM, eating straight from the chocolate ice cream tub. Because obviously, **chocolate fixes everything.**

2. The Family Function Food Trap

A big Indian gathering = food overload.

You're already anxious because:

o   Someone WILL comment on your weight.

o   Someone WILL ask about your past/ career/ kids/ marriage.

o   Someone WILL say, *"You've changed so much! I almost didn't recognize you!"* (What does that even mean?!)

To cope, you **overeat.** You tell yourself, *"It's just one day!"* But deep down, you know it's part of the cycle.

3. The Late-Night "Overthinking = Overeating" Syndrome

It's 1 AM. You're in bed. Your brain decides this is the **perfect time** to replay embarrassing moments from childhood.

What do you do? You **walk to the kitchen**, grab some leftover biryani, and **eat directly from the container** like a Bollywood villain plotting revenge.

How to Break the Cycle (Without Giving Up Your Favorite Foods)

o **Pause Before Eating:**

o Ask yourself: *Am I actually hungry, or just anxious?* If you wouldn't eat a plain roti, you're probably not actually hungry.

o **Find Other Comfort Mechanisms:**

o Instead of food, try a **quick walk, journaling, dancing to some great song or deep breathing**. (I know, not as exciting as samosas, but it helps.)

o **Drink Water First:**

o Sometimes thirst **pretends to be hunger**. Have a glass of water. If you're still hungry after 10 minutes, then eat. A chamomile tea may help in calming down

o **Use the "Small Plate" Trick:**

o Instead of eating from a giant serving bowl (we've all done it), serve yourself **on a small plate**. Your brain still thinks you're eating a full portion.

o **Don't Keep Trigger Foods in the House:**

o If chips aren't in the kitchen, you won't eat them at 2 AM. (But let's be real, this one is hard.)

o **Forgive Yourself and Move On:**

o You *will* mess up sometimes. The key is to **not** spiral into guilt and self-loathing. Just reset and try again.

Final Thoughts: Your Stomach Is Not Your Enemy

Anxiety and binge eating are a **messy duo**, but the good news? You're not alone, and it's **not impossible to fix**.

Next time your brain tries to convince you that **food is the only solution**, take a deep breath, pause, and ask yourself:

"Do I really need this, or is my anxiety just being dramatic?"

And if you still decide to eat that extra piece of cake? *Enjoy it.* But don't let it control you.

Sleep? What's That?

Ah, sleep. That beautiful, mysterious, almost mythical concept that some lucky people seem to experience every night. They close their eyes, drift into dreamland, and wake up refreshed, ready to conquer the world.

And then there's **us**—the anxious overthinkers, the night owls not by choice but by **compulsion**, the ones who experience sleep like a badly made Bollywood movie:

o **One night, it's a full-blown action thriller.** (Tossing, turning, fighting imaginary enemies in our head.)

o **Another night, it's a horror show.** (Vivid nightmares, waking up in a panic.)

o **Some nights, it's an emotional drama.** (Dreams so detailed and intense that you wake up crying, only to realize nothing actually happened.)

o **And then there are the mystery nights**—where you wake up **more tired than when you slept,** as if someone borrowed your body and ran a marathon while you were unconscious.

Basically, if sleep were a relationship, it would be the most **toxic** one ever. It plays **hard to get**, gives **mixed signals**, and leaves us feeling **confused, exhausted, and slightly betrayed** every morning.

Let's dive into the **chaos that is our sleep cycle.**

The Great Hide-and-Seek Game with Sleep

Sleep loves playing games. And its favorite game? **Hide-and-seek.**

Night 1: Hide Mode (a.k.a Insomnia Attack)

You get into bed early, determined to have a good night's sleep. You dim the lights, put away your phone, and close your eyes.

Your brain: *LOL, nice try.*

Now begins **Overthinking Season**—your personal brain theatre featuring:

o **A highlight reel of every embarrassing moment of your life.** (*Why did I say that dumb thing in 2008?*)

o **A sudden urge to analyze every decision you've ever made.** (*Did I really need to quit that job?*)

o **A deep dive into useless existential questions.** (*What is time? Are we all just floating in space?*)

o **The fear of the alarm clock.** (*If I sleep now, I'll get exactly 5 hours, 22 minutes, and 37 seconds of sleep… oh wait, now it's 5 hours, 21 minutes… Oh no, I'm panicking, I CAN'T SLEEP!*)

Before you know it, it's **4 AM** and you're wide awake, staring at the ceiling, questioning your entire existence.

Night 2: Seek Mode (a.k.a The Sleep Hangover)

After a sleepless night, you're running on fumes the next day. By noon, you look like a **zombie on a diet**—eyes half-closed, body moving in slow motion, brain functioning at 10%.

At work, people keep asking: **"Are you okay? You look tired."** (*Gee, thanks.*)

By evening, you're so drowsy you could pass out anywhere—standing in a queue, sitting in a rickshaw, or mid-conversation with your husband.

By 8 PM, your body is **BEGGING** for sleep. But guess what? The moment you lie down…

BOOM! FULL ENERGY ACTIVATED

It's like your body is a phone that charges in **two minutes flat**, and suddenly, you're wide awake, binge-watching reels or making imaginary speeches for situations that will never happen.

The Drama of Dreams

On the rare nights you **do** sleep, it's never peaceful. Nope. You get treated to a **Bollywood-level dream production**.

1. The Vivid Dream Saga

Ever had a dream so **detailed** and **realistic** that when you wake up, you actually **feel emotions** from it?

o   You dream you're fighting with a friend. Wake up **angry** at them.

o   You dream you won a lottery. Wake up **disappointed** that your bank balance is still struggling.

o   You dream of eating a giant dessert buffet. Wake up **hungry** and craving chocolate mousse at 3 AM.

2. The Horror Show

And then there are **nightmares**—those delightful productions where your brain decides to **traumatize you for no reason**.

- o   Ghosts? **Check.**

- o   Being chased by something unknown? **Check.**

- o   Teeth falling out? **Double check.**

- o   Missing an important exam you didn't even sign up for? **Of course.**

You wake up in a **panic**, heart racing, sweating, gasping for breath. You tell yourself *it was just a dream*, but your body **refuses to calm down** for another 30 minutes.

Why, brain, WHY?

The Curse of Hyperawareness

Another fun thing about anxiety? It makes you **hyperaware** even when you're trying to sleep.

- o   Any tiny sound = potential **life-threatening danger.**

- o   A random dog barking outside = definitely a **sign from the universe.**

- o   Your husband moving slightly = *"why is he breathing so hoarsely? Should we get him checked?*

- o   Your own heartbeat = *"Is that normal? Am I having palpitations?"*

Basically, your body refuses to **fully relax** because it's **constantly scanning for threats** like an overworked security guard.

Indian Household Sleep Problems

As if anxiety wasn't bad enough, **Indian households** come with their own set of sleep disturbances:

1. The Relatives Who Don't Believe in Time

Just about to sleep? Great! That's when some long-lost **mama, chacha, or bua** will call for a random chat.

Because in India, **there's no such thing as "late night" when it comes to relatives.**

2. The Alarm Olympics: Indian Household Edition

Who needs roosters when you have family members with five alarms each? My husband sets his first alarm at 5:00 a.m.—not to wake up, but to snooze. Then comes the 5:07 one, followed by 5:15, 5:22, 5:30... and so on, until 5:40 a.m., when he finally rushes to get to this workout session like a tornado in the room. My teenage daughter follows suit, with a musical medley of BTS alarm tones blaring every 10 minutes. Meanwhile, my son has five alarms but absolutely not perturbed to even get up and switch them off!!

And me? I'm wide awake by 4:55 a.m. with my set of alarms, not because I need to be, but because I live here. Sleep isn't just lost—**it's attacked, ambushed, and annihilated in this household warzone of alarms.**

3. The Ultimate Sleep Killer: Guilt

Indian parents believe that **sleeping in = laziness.**

If you wake up late (which is once in a purple moon kind of event), expect comments like:

o   *"What will you do in life if you can't even wake up on time?"*

o   *"Are you not well? Why are you sleeping so much?"*

o   *"Beta, good people wake up early and do some pranayam."*

Now you're **not just sleep-deprived, you're also emotionally damaged.**

How to Fix This Mess (Or At Least Try)

Look, I won't promise you a **perfect sleep schedule** because let's be real, our brains have other plans. But here are some things that might *help*:

o **Avoid caffeine after 5 PM.** (Chai lovers, I know this hurts.)

o **Put your phone away an hour before bed.** (Or at least stop reading WhatsApp forwards that send you into existential panic.)

o **Try a "brain dump" before bed.** Write down your thoughts so your brain doesn't need to replay them at 2 AM. (This really helps)

o **If you can't sleep, don't just lie there panicking.** Get up, read a book, or do something boring until you feel sleepy again.

o **Background noise helps.** White noise, rain sounds, or even an old TV serial playing softly in the background (*Mahabharat* reruns, anyone?).

Final Thoughts: Sleep Will Always Be a Struggle

Sleep is like that flaky friend who keeps canceling plans—**just when you think you've got it, it disappears again.**

But instead of fighting it, let's just **accept the madness.**

Some nights will be **sleepless torture**, some will be **random emotional rollercoasters**, and some will actually be **peaceful (rare, but it happens).**

And until sleep decides to be more consistent, let's survive on **power naps, smoothies, and a questionable amount of willpower.**

Breathing Like a Human Being: A Survival Guide for the Anxiously Inclined

Breathing—it's the **one thing we're supposed to do automatically**, yet somehow, when anxiety kicks in, even that turns into a disaster. Suddenly, your **lungs forget their job,** your chest tightens, and you're left wondering: *Am I breathing too fast? Too slow? Am I even breathing at all?!*

Congratulations! You have officially entered **The Anxiety Breath Spiral**—where one second you're fine, and the next, your own breath is sending you into full-blown panic mode.

The Great Breathing Disaster: How Anxiety Messes Up Your Lungs

When anxiety strikes, your breathing goes from **"calm and effortless"** to **"chaotic and confusing"** in a matter of seconds. And because your breath is directly connected to your **nervous system**, things start going downhill fast:

o   **The Tight Chest Situation** – Your chest suddenly feels like someone tied a **Rakhi around it too tightly**, making every breath feel like a struggle.

o   **The Sinking Feeling** – Your stomach drops like you just **missed a step on the stairs**, except you're sitting perfectly still.

o   **The Sudden Heartburn** – Your stomach, already an overachiever in the stress department, starts **throwing acid reflux into the mix**, just for fun.

Now, your brain, being the absolute *genius* that it is, **overreacts immediately.** Instead of recognizing this as anxiety messing with your breathing, it jumps to the worst-case scenario:

o *Oh no, is this a heart attack?*

o *What if I stop breathing completely?*

o *Should I Google "why does my chest feel weird"?*

Spoiler alert: **DO NOT GOOGLE IT.** The internet will convince you that you have **every disease known to mankind.**

The Breath-Anxiety Loop: How Your Own Body Betrays You

Here's the kicker—**your brain and breath are best friends.** They talk to each other *all the time.* So when anxiety speeds up your breathing, your brain **panics even more,** making your breath even worse.

This creates a **vicious cycle:**

o **You feel anxious.**

o **Your breath becomes shallow.**

o **Your brain notices and freaks out.**

o **Your breath becomes even more chaotic.**

o **Now you're convinced something is terribly wrong.**

This cycle can go on for **minutes, hours, or even days**, leaving you exhausted, confused, and in desperate need of a snack.

Breaking the Breath-Anxiety Cycle: Simple Hacks That Actually Work

Okay, now that we've established that your breath is your own worst enemy during anxiety, let's talk about **how to fix it.** The good news? **You CAN take back control.** The even better news? **It's easier than you think.**

1. The "I'm Not Dying, I Just Need to Breathe" Trick

First things first—Talk to yourself!!...**remind yourself that nothing bad is happening.** You are **not suffocating, not having a heart attack, and not going to collapse dramatically like in a Bollywood movie.** Your body is just **freaking out unnecessarily.**

2. The 4-7-8 Method (The Cheat Code for Your Lungs)

If anxiety has turned your breathing into a **chaotic mess**, this is the **reset button you need:**

- o **Inhale for 4 seconds** (deep but gentle).

- o **Hold for 7 seconds** (let the oxygen do its thing).

- o **Exhale slowly for 8 seconds** (like blowing out a birthday candle in slow motion).

This technique **forces your nervous system to chill out.** Do it 5-6 times, and you'll feel **a little more human again.**

3. The "Breathe Like a Baby" Hack

Ever noticed how babies breathe? **Their stomachs expand when they inhale and relax when they exhale.** That's **how we're supposed to breathe.**

But thanks to years of stress, we've all started **breathing from our chest** instead. This leads to **shallow, panic-inducing breaths.**

Here's how to **fix it:**

- o **Put one hand on your chest and the other on your belly.**

- o **Breathe in deeply and make sure your belly moves more than your chest.**

- o **Exhale slowly and feel your stomach drop back down.**

This **immediately signals** to your brain: *Hey, we're safe. No need for panic mode.*

4. The "Lambi Saans Lo, Beta" Technique (Because Moms Are Always Right)

Indian moms **love telling us to take deep breaths** whenever we're stressed. Turns out, **they were onto something.**

A **simple deep breath** (inhale deeply through the nose, hold for 2 seconds, and exhale slowly) can **instantly reduce anxiety levels**. Plus, you get to tell your mom she was right. Win-win.

5. The "Get Moving Before Your Brain Overthinks" Rule

Sometimes, **fixing your breath isn't about breathing at all.** It's about **moving** before your brain gets stuck in an anxiety loop.

- o **Take a brisk 5-minute walk.**
- o **Stretch your arms and shoulders.**
- o **Do a few jumping jacks (yes, really).**
- o **Shake your hands like you're drying them without a towel.**

These movements **force your body to reset**, so your breath follows suit.

Why Fixing Your Breath Is the Key to Fixing Anxiety

At the end of the day, **your breath is the remote control for your nervous system.** If you learn to control your breathing, you can **literally** switch your body from **panic mode to calm mode.**

Here's why:

- o **Slow, deep breaths = Telling your brain "We're safe."**
- o **Shallow, rapid breaths = Telling your brain "PANIC! SOMETHING IS WRONG!"**

The moment you take charge of your breathing, **your brain stops spiraling.** It's like calming down a hyperactive child—**once you soothe it, everything else falls into place.**

Final Thoughts: Breathe, Laugh, and Keep Going

Anxiety will try **every trick in the book** to mess with your breath. But now, you **know better.** You have the hacks, the techniques, and most importantly, the knowledge that **you are NOT broken.**

So the next time anxiety hijacks your lungs, just remember:

o   **You are NOT dying.**

o   **Your breath is just being dramatic.**

o   **You have the power to reset it.**

Now, take a deep breath, relax, and maybe go treat yourself to a snack. **You survived another anxiety attack like a boss.**

The Gut-Brain Connection: How Food Impacts Anxiety (And Why Your Stomach is Basically a Drama Queen)

If you've ever eaten an entire pizza in one sitting and then felt like **the universe was collapsing around you,** congratulations! You've just witnessed **the gut-brain connection in action.**

Most people think **anxiety lives in the brain**, but what if I told you that **your stomach is the actual villain** behind many of your worst overthinking spirals? Your gut and brain are in **constant communication**, like two gossiping aunties at a wedding. If your gut is happy, your brain feels relaxed. But if your gut is upset? **Oh boy, brace yourself for some world-class overreactions.**

So, if you want to manage your **anxiety, panic attacks, or general tendency to turn small problems into full-blown crises,** you need to **start with your gut.** Let's break it down.

Your Gut & Brain Are Secretly Besties (And Also a Bit Toxic)

Imagine your **gut and brain as two best friends who share everything.** If one is feeling low, the other gets affected too.

Here's how it works:

o   Your gut is filled with **trillions of bacteria** (yes, you are basically a human-sized petri dish).

o   These bacteria help in **digesting food, absorbing nutrients, and producing brain chemicals** like serotonin and dopamine—the same ones that keep you sane.

o   In fact, **90% of serotonin (your "happy hormone") is produced in the gut, not the brain.**

o   If your gut bacteria are balanced and healthy, **you feel calmer, happier, and more in control.**

o   But if your gut is a mess—thanks to junk food, stress, or skipping meals—**your brain starts panicking** for no reason.

So, next time you find yourself **spiraling into an overthinking loop about why your friend hasn't replied to your WhatsApp message,** ask yourself:

"Is this really about my friend? Or is it because I had three cups of coffee and no proper meal today?"

The Worst Foods for Anxiety: What NOT to Eat

Now that we know your gut controls your mood, let's talk about the real **culprits behind gut-induced anxiety.**

1. Dairy Products: A Cocktail of Stress Hormones

You know how people say **"Milk makes you strong"**? Well, they forgot to mention that it also comes loaded with **stress hormones from the cow.**

Think about it—cows are **forced to produce milk nonstop**, and they go through **massive amounts of stress** in the process. That stress releases **cortisol (the stress hormone),** which then **ends up in your glass of milk, your cheese, or your butter toast.**

Now, if you're already an anxious person, drinking milk is like **inviting more drama into your life for no reason.** If you've ever felt **bloated, sluggish, or randomly irritated after dairy, now you know why.**

2. Animal Products: The Secret Anxiety Triggers

Let's be real—when an animal is about to be slaughtered, it's not exactly **meditating peacefully.** It's terrified, which means its body releases **tons of stress hormones like cortisol and adrenaline.**

And guess where those hormones go?

Right into your chicken curry, mutton biryani, or fish fry.

So, when you eat meat, you're not just getting protein—you're also **absorbing all the stress and fear that the animal went through.** If you're already prone to overthinking, meat is just **adding fuel to the fire.**

3. Refined Sugar: The Sweetest Anxiety Trap

Ah, sugar. The ultimate **toxic ex** who keeps coming back into your life, making false promises.

o   You eat sugar → You feel a short-term dopamine high → You feel happy.

o   But then… blood sugar crashes →You feel moody, irritable, and anxious.

It's like going on a **terrible date that started great but ended with you questioning all your life choices.**

Instead of refined sugar, go for **natural sweets like dates, jaggery, or fruit.** Your gut will thank you, and your brain won't make you cry at 2 AM for no reason.

4. Caffeine: The Official Sponsor of Panic Attacks

Look, I get it. Coffee is life. But if you're an anxious person, **coffee is NOT your best friend.**

Caffeine:

o   Increases **cortisol** (stress hormone)

o   Makes your **heart race**

o   Triggers **overthinking**

o   **Mimics the symptoms of a panic attack** (racing heart, jitteriness, breathlessness)

So, if you already wake up feeling **like life is an exam you forgot to prepare for,** maybe switch to **green tea, chamomile tea, or coconut water** instead of coffee.

5. Processed Junk Food: Your Gut's Worst Nightmare

If it comes in a shiny packet and has **ingredients you can't pronounce,** it's probably messing with your gut.

o   Artificial preservatives → Mess up gut bacteria

o   Excess salt & oil → Cause inflammation

o   Added chemicals → Increase stress on the digestive system

If you eat **instant noodles, chips, or biscuits regularly,** your gut is probably in **a toxic relationship with your brain.** Try replacing them with **homemade snacks, nuts, or fruit** instead.

The Best Foods for Anxiety: What to Eat More Of

Now that we've eliminated the **gut-destroying villains,** let's talk about the **mood-boosting superheroes.**

1. Fermented Foods: Your Gut's Best Friends

Fermented foods contain **probiotics (good bacteria)** that help balance your gut and calm your brain. Try including:

- o   **Dairy-free curd** (coconut curd, peanut curd)

- o   **Idli, dosa, and fermented batters**

- o   **Kanji (fermented carrot drink)**

- o   **Kimchi, Sauerkraut, Miso** (if you're feeling fancy)

2. Leafy Greens: Natural Anxiety Medicine

Spinach, methi (fenugreek), and coriander are **rich in magnesium**, which helps relax nerves and reduce anxiety.

Pro Tip: Throw greens into **dal, smoothies, or rotis** to make them less boring.

A green smoothie a day keeps the doctor away.

3. Nuts & Seeds: Tiny but Mighty Stress Busters

- o   **Walnuts & Almonds** → Rich in omega-3, which fights anxiety.

- o   **Flaxseeds & Chia Seeds** → Boost serotonin (your happy hormone).

- o   **Pumpkin Seeds** → High in magnesium, helps with relaxation.

4. Fruits: Nature's Candy & Mood Booster

Bananas, oranges, and mangoes are packed with **fiber, vitamins, and antioxidants** to keep your gut and mood stable.

5. Herbal Teas: The Anti-Anxiety Elixirs

Instead of coffee, try:

o **Chamomile tea** ☒ Naturally calming, great for sleep.

o **Ashwagandha tea** ☒ Lowers stress and anxiety.

o **Peppermint tea** ☒ Soothes digestion and reduces gut-related anxiety.

Final Thoughts: Feed Your Gut, Calm Your Mind

If you want to **reduce anxiety**, start with **fixing your gut.**

o Cut out **dairy, meat, sugar, caffeine, and processed junk.**

o Eat more **fermented foods, greens, nuts, and fruits.**

o Swap coffee for **herbal teas.**

o And most importantly—**don't stress about food too much.**

Your gut and brain should be **best friends, not toxic roommates.** So, start treating them with **kindness, good food, and lots of laughter.**

Now, go grab a smoothie, munch on some nuts, and **watch your anxiety levels drop like a bad internet connection.**

Chapter 3

Eating Habits of the Anxious

Stress Eating vs. Starving: The Two Extremes

There are two types of anxious eaters: the **"devour everything in sight" stress eater** and the **"forget food exists" starver**. I, being an overachiever (thanks, anxiety), manage to be both—just depends on what's stressing me out.

Work stress? Relationship woes? A general lack of TLC? I'm reaching for pani puri like my life depends on it.

Financial worries? Health concerns? Oh no, food? What is that? Why does my stomach feel like an empty abyss?

And then, of course, there's the **"special guest appearance" of my menstrual cycle**, which decides whether my stress eating will turn into an all-you-can-eat binge fest or if I'll just sit in a corner, surviving on coconut water and existential dread.

But here's the catch—I'm a **whole-food, plant-based nutritionist**, which means I *know* what I should be eating. I *teach* people what to eat. And yet, when anxiety comes knocking, my stomach does **exactly what it wants**.

Let's dive into these two extremes, shall we?

1. Stress Eating: Pani Puri, Vada Pav, and Other Love Affairs

Stress eating is basically my **coping mechanism in food form**. When something goes wrong, my first instinct isn't to *breathe* or *meditate*—no, no. My brain says, "Find food. Now."

A perfect example? **Gratitude Kitchen stress.**

Now, I love my cloud kitchen, but running it means **daily mini heart attacks**—staff issues, ingredient shortages, customer complaints, orders going out late. And let's not forget the ultimate horror: **a bad review.**

The moment anxiety kicks in, I don't crave a *wholesome Buddha bowl* or *a green smoothie*. Nope. My body is like: **"Fried. Spicy. Street food. Now."**

That's how I find myself standing outside a pani puri stall, **justifying my life choices.**

Me: *"Listen, this is wheat-based. Whole grains. The potato is complex carbs. The water has tamarind—good for digestion. The chickpeas? Protein. The sev… okay, let's ignore the sev."*

My stomach: *"Shhh. Just eat."*

And let's not even talk about **vada pav**—the ultimate comfort food. Something about that spicy chutney and deep-fried potato patty between a soft bun makes me forget that my kitchen just ran out of tofu for the fourth time this week.

Of course, **guilt follows immediately**. My nutritionist brain wakes up *after* the damage is done.

Brain: *"Congratulations. You just inhaled 500 calories of oil and refined carbs. Happy now?"*

Me: *"No. But also, yes."*

2. The "Forget to Eat" Starvation Mode

Now, let's talk about the **opposite**.

When the stress is related to **finances or health**, my stomach **shuts down completely.**

For example, let's say I have an upcoming **SHARAN India workshop**. Instead of thinking, *"Oh great, I get to educate people on plant-based nutrition!"*, my anxiety says:

o   *"What if no one shows up?"*

o   *"What if I forget something important?"*

o   *"What if the internet crashes mid-presentation?"*

o   *"What if I say something dumb and someone records it and it goes viral for the wrong reasons?"*

And before I know it, I've **skipped breakfast and lunch** without even realizing it.

By the time I'm done with the workshop, my body finally remembers it hasn't been fed in **12 hours**. And then, of course, the **realization hits like a truck**:

Me: *"I am STARVING."*

My stomach: *"And whose fault is that?"*

At this point, I have **two options**:

o   **Eat something nutritious** and get back on track.

o   **Eat an entire bag of roasted peanuts and call it dinner.**

Unfortunately, if I've **skipped too many meals**, my stomach just **stays confused**—like, *"Do we eat now? Do we wait? Should we just give up?"*

3. The Menstrual Cycle: The Wild Card

Now, just when I think I understand my eating patterns, **my period** enters the chat and says:

"Oh, you think you have control? That's cute."

Depending on my cycle, my stress eating can **turn into full-blown bingeing** or my appetite can **disappear completely**.

One week, I'm **eating an entire jar of peanut butter with a spoon** because *"it's protein, okay?"*

The next, I'm **living off lemon water** because everything else feels *too much*.

The worst part? The **cravings make no sense.**

One month, I might be **obsessed with mangoes**—cut, blended, raw, anything. The next month, mangoes **disgust me**, and I only want crispy masala dosa.

It's **chaos**, and I just have to **ride the wave.**

4. My Daughter: The Voice of Reason

Now, in the middle of all this **food chaos**, my **14-year-old daughter** somehow manages to be **the stable one.**

Me: *«I'm stressed. I need chocolate."*

Daughter: *"No, you need watermelon. It's hydrating and full of antioxidants."*

Me: *"Watermelon is NOT chocolate."*

Daughter: *"And yet, you'll feel better after eating it."*

And the worst part? **She's right.**

While I'm losing my mind over **pani puri cravings and starvation episodes**, she's over there making **perfectly balanced smoothies and snacks**—even when she's stressed about school.

It's humbling. And slightly annoying.

5. Tips to Manage Anxiety-Induced Eating Patterns

So, after **years of battling stress eating and accidental starvation**, here are a few tricks that actually help:

o **Pre-plan "safe" comfort foods**

1. When I'm stressed, I **will** eat something indulgent. So, I keep **healthy(ish) versions** of my cravings ready.

2. Instead of vada pav, I make **baked sweet potato chaat**.

3. Instead of pani puri, I make **homemade baked whole-wheat puris with toppings**.

4. It's not the same, but it **tricks my brain** enough.

o **Set meal reminders**

1. When I'm stressed, I **forget to eat**. So, I set alarms for meals.

2. If my phone says "Lunch Time", I force myself to grab a bowl of something—even if it's just a smoothie.

o **Hydrate first, eat second**

1. **Dehydration makes anxiety** worse.

2. Half the time, I think I'm craving food, but **I just need water or coconut water**.

o **Practice the "5-Minute Rule" for bingeing**

1. When I get the **urge to stress eat**, I tell myself: «Wait five minutes.»

2. In those five minutes, I drink **water or walk around**.

3. If I **still want the food**, I eat it. But most of the time, the craving **passes**.

o **Let go of guilt**

1. Stress eating happens. Starving happens.

2. The key is to notice it, accept it, and **course-correct the next meal**—without self-hate.

Final Thoughts

Anxiety and food have **a very complicated relationship**. Some days, I'm stuffing my face with pani puri. Other days, I'm running on **air and adrenaline**.

But through trial and error (and my very **wise teenager**), I've learned that **awareness is the first step**.

So, if you find yourself **mindlessly munching or skipping meals**, just take a deep breath and ask:

"Am I actually hungry, or is this just my anxiety talking?"

(And if the answer is **pani puri**, at least try to make it at home.)

Food as Comfort, Food as Fear

If you've been reading this book and thinking, *"Wow, this woman is anxious 24/7!"*, let me reassure you—that's **not true**. I have some **fantastic days** where I'm calm, productive, and in full control of my life. I also have **some struggle days**, where I'm just trying to survive and not let my anxiety spiral into a full-blown Bollywood-style meltdown.

But the tricky part with anxiety is that you **never know when it's going to hit**—or how intense it's going to be. One day, I'm fine. The next day, a slightly upheaval has me questioning every life decision I've ever made.

Now, while I do have some solid **coping mechanisms** (which we will talk about later), there's **one thing that's always been my quickest and most accessible form of comfort—food**.

Food doesn't judge. It doesn't give you **wrong replies** or ignore your texts. It doesn't roll its eyes at you when you overthink things. Food is just... **there**—ready to offer warmth, comfort, and a delicious distraction from whatever emotional hurricane is brewing inside.

But food can also be a **response to fear**—an escape, a flight response. Instead of facing whatever is making me anxious, I can just **distract myself with a plate of something delicious**.

Let's talk about **both sides** of this complicated relationship with food.

Food as Comfort: The Ultimate Emotional Support System

If food had a LinkedIn profile, under "Skills & Expertise," it would say:

- ✓ Instant Mood Lifter

- ✓ Expert in Hugs Without Physical Contact

- ✓ Distraction from Real-Life Problems

Some days, **life is just hard**, and I need something warm, delicious, and familiar to **wrap me in its metaphorical arms**. And when that happens, my **brain automatically goes into "comfort food" mode**.

A bad day at work? I need **a bowl of hot dal-chawal**—the culinary equivalent of being wrapped in a cozy blanket.

An argument with my husband? Give me **a plate of rajma chawal**, and suddenly, life feels more manageable.

Overwhelmed with responsibilities? **Garam vegan chai and pakoras**, because if I'm drowning in stress, I might as well drown it in masala and fried goodness.

Food has this **magical ability** to make everything feel okay, even if it's just for a little while. And honestly, sometimes that little while is **exactly what I need** to regain my balance.

But—and there's always a *but*—**there's a flip side to this relationship**.

Food as Fear: The Flight Response in Action

Now, while comfort eating is **one side** of the equation, there's another aspect that most people don't talk about—**eating out of fear**.

Sometimes, anxiety doesn't just make me reach for food for comfort—it makes me use food as a **shield**. Instead of **facing my fear**, I **bury myself in food** to **avoid dealing with reality**.

And nowhere was this more evident than during **my stroke days**.

The Stroke, The Fear, and The Food

When I had my **stroke**, my entire world turned **upside down overnight**. My senses were compromised, my motor functions weren't cooperating, and my body felt **foreign** to me.

It was terrifying.

And in that **state of fear and helplessness**, I turned to **food**.

Why? Because **food was something I could still control.**

- I couldn't control how my body was reacting, but I could **decide what to eat.**

- I couldn't predict how long it would take to recover, but I could **find temporary comfort in flavors and textures.**

- I couldn't process the emotional trauma of what had happened, so instead, I **focused on my next meal.**

But here's where it got tricky—**was I eating because I was actually hungry, or was I eating because I didn't want to deal with my emotions?**

The answer? A little bit of both.

Food became a way to avoid sitting with my fear. If I was **eating**, I wasn't thinking. If I was **focused on what to eat next**, I wasn't focused on the **"what ifs"** running through my head.

And that's when I realized—sometimes, we don't just **eat to feel better**. We **eat to escape.**

The Indian Culture Factor: Food as Love, Food as Expectation

Now, in Indian culture, food is more than just **nourishment**—it's **love, emotion, tradition, and sometimes, obligation.**

- Your mom expresses love by asking, *"Beta, aur roti loge?"*

- Your dadi's version of therapy is **stuffing you with ghee-laden parathas.**

- Your relatives will literally **guilt-trip you for eating too little—** *"Bas? Itna hi khaoge? Bimar ho kya?"*

So, when food is so deeply tied to **love and relationships**, it's no surprise that it becomes our **go-to emotional crutch.**

But there's also **the flip side—food as expectation.**

There's an **unspoken rule** that if you're at a social gathering, you **must eat enthusiastically**, or risk offending the host.

This has led to **many awkward moments**:

Me (at a relative's house, already full): *"Bas thoda sa, aunty."*

Aunty: *"Thoda sa? Yeh kya hota hai? Aloo puri toh kha lo!"*

Me: *"Nahi, bas ek—»*

Aunty (already piling more food on my plate): *"Ek nahi, do lo!"*

And just like that, I've eaten **an entire meal's worth of food I didn't want**—not out of hunger, not out of comfort, but out of **social obligation.**

So, What's the Solution? Finding the Balance

Through all of this, I've learned one important thing—**awareness is key.**

- If I'm **eating for comfort**, I make sure it's **mindful and not just a distraction**.

- If I'm **eating out of fear**, I take a moment to ask myself, *"What am I avoiding?"*

- If I'm **being guilt-tripped into eating**, I remind myself that **it's okay to say no.**

And most importantly—I've started listening to **my body** instead of just **my emotions.**

Because at the end of the day, food should be **enjoyed,** not used as an escape route.

Final Thoughts: Food is a Friend, Not a Therapist

Look, I **love food.** I run a **vegan cloud kitchen**, I'm a **plant-based nutritionist**, and I genuinely enjoy **good meals.** But food is **not my therapist**—it can't solve my problems.

So, while I still turn to **dal-chawal on bad days**, I also remind myself that **real comfort comes from facing my emotions, not just eating through them.**

And if all else fails—there's always **a wonderful smoothie !.**

The Power of Whole Plant-Based Eating in Healing Anxiety

Let's be honest—when we think about managing anxiety, food isn't the first thing that comes to mind. Meditation? Yes. Yoga? Of course. Deep breathing? Definitely. But diet? Most people don't make the connection.

I used to be one of those people. For years, I thought my anxiety had nothing to do with my plate. I believed it was just a **default setting** in my brain—like those annoying pre-installed apps on your phone that you can't delete.

But over time, I realized that **what I eat plays a huge role in how I feel—mentally and emotionally.** Food isn't just about **calories and nutrition**; it's about **mood, hormones, and brain function.**

And let me tell you—**a whole-food, plant-based diet** has been a game-changer for my anxiety.

Wait, What Does Food Have to Do with Anxiety?

Imagine you just drank **three cups of coffee** on an empty stomach. Your hands are shaking, your heart is racing, and you're suddenly convinced that you forgot to lock the door, reply to an important email, and maybe even feed the cat (even if you don't own one).

That's your nervous system **on overdrive.**

Now imagine eating a **big, greasy meal loaded with dairy and processed junk.** You feel sluggish, bloated, and heavy—not just in your stomach, but in your mind. Your energy crashes, your mood dips, and suddenly, you're snapping at your family because someone left the toothpaste cap off.

That's your **gut-brain connection** in action.

Your gut and brain are **constantly communicating**, and what you eat **directly affects your mental state.**

A plant-based diet—rich in whole, unprocessed foods—**supports** your nervous system instead of **overloading it.** It helps you feel **calmer, more balanced, and in control**—which, if you have anxiety, is basically the dream.

Why Whole Plant-Based Foods Help with Anxiety

Let's break it down.

1. A Happy Gut = A Happy Mind

Did you know that **90% of serotonin (your "feel-good" neurotransmitter) is produced in your gut**? If your gut is unhappy, your brain is unhappy.

Whole plant-based foods—like fruits, vegetables, legumes, and whole grains—**feed the good bacteria in your gut**. This leads to **better digestion, less inflammation, and improved mood regulation**.

On the other hand, animal products and processed foods can **disrupt gut health**, leading to mood swings, brain fog, and—you guessed it—**more anxiety**.

2. Bye-Bye, Stress Hormones from Animal Products

Ever heard the phrase *"You are what you eat"*? Well, if you're eating **stressed-out animals**, you're also eating **their stress hormones**.

Animals raised for food experience **extreme stress** before they are slaughtered, and that stress releases hormones like **cortisol and adrenaline**—the same hormones that flood your body when you're anxious.

So when you consume **meat, dairy, and eggs**, you're literally adding more **stress hormones** into your system.

Switching to **plant-based foods** removes that extra burden on your body, making it **easier to stay calm and balanced**.

3. No More Blood Sugar Rollercoaster

Ever felt **jittery, irritable, or lightheaded** because you skipped a meal? Or experienced a **post-lunch crash** after eating something sugary? That's **blood sugar fluctuation**, and it's a nightmare for anxiety.

Refined carbs, sugar, and processed foods make your blood sugar **spike and crash**, which makes your **mood unstable**. One moment you're fine, and the next you're having an existential crisis over a missing sock.

Whole plant-based foods—like **quinoa, lentils, and sweet potatoes—** keep blood sugar **steady**, which helps keep your **mood stable**.

4. Magnesium = The Chill Pill

If anxiety had a natural enemy, it would be **magnesium**.

Magnesium is a **powerful relaxant**, and it's found in **leafy greens, nuts, seeds, and whole grains**—all plant-based foods.

Most people are **deficient in magnesium**, which makes them feel more **stressed, restless, and on edge**. But when you eat a diet rich in **plant-based magnesium**, it's like giving your nervous system a warm hug.

(*Fun fact: Dark chocolate is high in magnesium. So if you ever needed an excuse to eat it, here you go!*).

5. Anti-Inflammatory Foods for a Calmer Mind

Inflammation is like that **toxic relative** who shows up uninvited and ruins the vibe. It's linked to **anxiety, depression, and brain fog**.

The good news? Whole plant-based foods are **naturally anti-inflammatory**.

Fruits, vegetables, nuts, seeds, and legumes help **reduce inflammation**, while dairy, meat, and processed foods make it worse.

So, if you want a **calmer, clearer mind**, eating **anti-inflammatory plant-based foods** is a great start.

My Personal Anxiety-Food Connection

I didn't always eat this way. There was a time when my diet looked like:

- Chai with **three spoons of sugar** to "wake up"

- Cheese toast as a "quick snack"

- Some **deep-fried goodness** whenever I was stressed

- A **post-dinner dessert** because "I deserve it"

And let me tell you—it **did not help my anxiety**.

After switching to a whole-food, plant-based diet, I **noticed real changes**:

- **My panic attacks became less frequent.**
- **My energy was more stable.**
- **I felt lighter, both physically and mentally.**
- **I slept better.**

And the best part? **I didn't feel deprived.** Plant-based food is **delicious** (if done right), and I still got to enjoy my **favorite comfort meals—just in healthier versions**.

Simple Food Swaps to Reduce Anxiety

Want to eat plant-based but don't know where to start? Here are some **easy swaps:**

Instead of This	Try This
Milk	Almond milk, oat milk, coconut milk
Paneer	Tofu or homemade cashew cheese
Ghee	Coconut oil or nut butter
Sugar-loaded chai	Herbal tea or green tea with date syrup
Deep-fried snacks	Roasted makhana, baked samosas. Air fried French fries
White rice	Quinoa, brown rice
Processed sweets	Dates, dark chocolate, fruit-based desserts

The goal is **not to be perfect—**it's to **make small, sustainable changes that help your mind and body feel better.**

Final Thoughts: Food as Medicine for the Mind

Switching to a whole-food, plant-based diet is **not a magic cure** for anxiety. But it's one of the most **powerful, natural tools** to support your mental health.

- It balances your **hormones**.

- It stabilizes your **mood**.

- It calms your **nervous system**.

And most importantly—it helps you **feel in control of your body and mind**.

So, if you struggle with anxiety, consider **starting with your plate**. The food you eat is **either fueling your anxiety or fighting it**—and I know which side I'd rather be on.

And if all else fails—just breathe, eat some **dark chocolate**, and remind yourself that **you've got this.**

Caffeine, Sugar, and Other Frenemies

If anxiety had a VIP guest list, caffeine and sugar would be right at the top, dressed to kill, ready to wreak havoc on your already jittery nervous system. And trust me, I would know—I was once their most loyal fan.

For years, I was practically a walking coffee bean. Sixteen cups a day? Child's play. If coffee had a loyalty program, I would have earned enough points for a lifetime supply. And let's not forget my childhood romance with that tiny, citrusy, artificially-colored 50-paise orange candy outside school. It was basically sugar, chemicals, and joy rolled into one. Then there was my mom's favorite dessert—jelly and custard—so loaded with processed sugar and artificial colors that it could probably glow in the dark.

But as much as I loved them, these so-called "treats" weren't exactly treating me well. They were playing mind games, pretending to comfort me while secretly fueling my anxiety. And it wasn't just them—turns out, our food is filled with sneaky little culprits that mess with our brains, our moods, and our already overactive stress responses.

So let's talk about some of the worst offenders—the fake friends in your diet who pretend to help but are actually making things worse.

Caffeine: The Friend Who Hypes You Up, Then Ghosts You

Caffeine and I had a toxic relationship. It made me feel invincible at first— like I could run 3 businesses, cook a five-course meal, and solve world hunger all before noon. But then, the crash came, and suddenly I was curled up in a corner questioning every life decision I had ever made.

Caffeine is basically an energy loan shark. It gives you a quick high, but you pay for it later—with interest. It overstimulates the nervous system, increases heart rate, and can make you feel like you're having a full-blown panic attack over something as simple as a WhatsApp message left on 'read.'

Anxious people often turn to coffee thinking it'll help them power through the day. Spoiler alert: It does the exact opposite. It hijacks your stress hormones, making sure your anxiety stays on edge like a Bollywood hero waiting for the villain to strike.

Signs caffeine is ruining your life:

- You feel energetic, but also like you might spontaneously combust.

- Your hands shake like you've just been asked to give a speech in front of 10,000 people.

- You're on your third cup and still feel exhausted.

- You wake up tired and go to bed wired.

Better Alternatives:

- Green tea: Has just enough caffeine to keep you awake but also contains L-theanine, which calms the nervous system.

- Herbal teas: Chamomile, lavender, or lemon balm can work wonders.

- Golden milk: Warm turmeric and plant-based milk with a little cinnamon—it's like a hug for your insides.

Sugar: The Sweet Assassin

Sugar is the ultimate backstabber. It gives you a quick serotonin rush, making you feel like life is all sunshine and rainbows—until the crash, when suddenly, everything is terrible, and you're crying because your internet is slow.

My love affair with sugar started young—with that glorious 50-paise orange candy outside school. It was pure, unadulterated joy in a wrapper. But little did I know, sugar was whispering sweet nothings to my dopamine receptors, getting me addicted to the high.

Sugar messes with your mood, increases inflammation, and turns your anxiety dial up to *maximum drama mode*. It gives you a temporary sense of comfort but leaves you feeling worse than before—like a bad rebound relationship.

The Sugar Cycle:

- You eat sugar. You feel great!

- Your blood sugar spikes. You're on top of the world!

- Blood sugar crashes. Now you hate everyone, including yourself.

- You crave more sugar to feel better again.

- Repeat forever.

Signs sugar is controlling your life:

- You feel happy for five minutes and then suddenly depressed.

- You crave sweets after every meal, like a ritual.

- You're constantly tired but wired at the same time.

Better Alternatives:

- Natural sweeteners like dates, jaggery, or maple syrup.

- Whole fruits—they have fiber, so they don't send your blood sugar on a roller coaster ride.

- Dark chocolate (at least 70% cocoa) for a healthy-ish treat.

MSG: The Sneaky Villain in Your Favorite Snacks

MSG (monosodium glutamate) is like that shady friend who pretends to be helpful but actually stirs up drama behind your back. It's in chips, instant noodles, Chinese takeout, and anything that tastes *too good to be true.*

MSG tricks your brain into thinking food is delicious and addictive. But it also overstimulates the nervous system, leading to *mood swings, headaches, and increased anxiety.* Ever wondered why you can't stop eating that packet of chips even though you're not hungry? Yep, blame MSG.

Signs MSG is messing with you:

- You eat a bag of chips and suddenly feel irritable for no reason.

- You get a headache after eating Chinese takeout.

- You feel bloated, sluggish, and anxious.

Better Alternatives:

- Make your own snacks at home with real ingredients.

- Choose brands that proudly say "No MSG added."

- Use herbs, nutritional yeast, and spices for flavor instead.

Artificial Sweeteners: The Fake Friends of the Food World

You thought sugar was bad? Meet its evil twin: artificial sweeteners. Aspartame, saccharin, sucralose—all these "zero-calorie" wonders promise weight loss and blood sugar control but come with a side of *anxiety, mood swings, and gut issues.*

Aspartame, in particular, has been linked to changes in brain chemistry, which can make anxious people even more anxious. Plus, these sweeteners trick your body into thinking it's getting sugar, leading to cravings, overeating, and—you guessed it—more anxiety.

Signs artificial sweeteners are ruining your life:

- You feel moody after a diet soda.

- Your sugar cravings actually increase after using them.

- You have digestive issues like bloating or discomfort.

Better Alternatives:

- Stick to natural sweeteners like dates, coconut sugar, or raw honey (if you're not vegan).

- Drink plain soda water with a squeeze of lemon instead of diet drinks.

- Eat whole fruits instead of anything labeled "sugar-free."

Food Coloring & Flavor Enhancers: The Makeup of the Food World

Ever wondered why some candies, cakes, and drinks have such *unnaturally bright* colors? That's artificial food coloring, baby! And it's doing more than just making your food look good—it's *messing with your mood, your gut, and your anxiety levels.*

Certain food dyes have been linked to hyperactivity, mood swings, and increased stress. Think of them as Instagram filters for food—pretty but completely fake.

Signs artificial colors are affecting you:

- You feel unusually restless after eating colorful junk food.

- You notice skin reactions or stomach issues.

- You have unexplained mood swings after eating processed foods.

Better Alternatives:

- Use natural colorants like beetroot powder, turmeric, or matcha.

- Eat fresh, unprocessed foods—nature already made them pretty!

- Read labels and avoid anything with "Red 40," "Yellow 5," or "Blue 1."

Final Thoughts: Break Up with These Frenemies

The food we eat has a *direct* impact on our anxiety. It can either support our nervous system or send it into full-blown panic mode. Cutting down on caffeine, sugar, MSG, artificial sweeteners, and food coloring might not solve *all* your problems, but it will make dealing with them a whole lot easier.

So the next time you reach for that diet soda or that MSG-laden snack, just ask yourself: *Do I really want this, or is my anxiety tricking me?* Because trust me—your mind and body will thank you for choosing real, whole, anxiety-friendly foods.

And if you ever feel like you need a hug from food, just eat a banana. They're rich in magnesium, serotonin-boosting, and don't ghost you like caffeine does.

Chapter 4

Self-Care or Self-Sabotage?

The Myth of "Relaxing" for Anxious People

For most people, "self-care" means lighting a scented candle, putting on a face mask, and sinking into a warm bath. Maybe even sipping on some chamomile tea while reading a book. Sounds peaceful, right?

For an anxious person, however, "self-care" is a full-blown, overanalysed, emotionally exhausting process that somehow leaves you feeling more stressed than before.

Take me, for example. I run a **vegan cloud kitchen**, raise **two kids**, have my classes and programs with SHARAN Indiatake **consultations to help people heal**, and somehow still manage to **overthink every tiny detail of life**. My version of self-care looks something like this:

o **Deciding to relax for 30 minutes.** Then spending 28 of those minutes thinking about all the things I *should* be doing instead.

o **Trying to meditate.** Only to get distracted by thoughts like, *Did I turn off the stove? Did my last WhatsApp message sound rude? Is my daughter really okay, or is she just pretending?*

o **Taking a break with Netflix.** But feeling guilty about wasting time, so I start multitasking and answering emails while pretending to enjoy the show.

The truth is, relaxation for an anxious person is an **extreme sport**—one that requires *strategy, commitment, and an inner pep talk that lasts longer than the relaxation itself.*

Attempt #1: The "Self-Care Sunday" Disaster

One Sunday, I decided I was going to have a proper self-care day. No work, no stress, just relaxation.

Step 1: I made a nice cup of herbal tea, hoping it would magically calm my nerves.

Step 2: I sat down with a book, thinking, *This is it. This is self-care.*

Step 3: Five minutes in, my brain started screaming:

o   *Did I reply to that client's message?*

o   *What if I don't get enough orders next week?*

o   *What if I get too many orders and can't manage?*

o   *Should I scale my business or keep it small?*

o   *What if my kids need me and I'm too busy?*

Before I knew it, my tea was cold, my book was unread, and I was pacing the room like a detective trying to crack a case. Self-care attempt: **FAILED.**

Attempt #2: The Spa Appointment That Gave Me a Panic Attack

Everyone told me, *"You need to go for a spa day. It will relax you."*

So, I booked a massage appointment, hoping to melt away all my stress. Instead, this is what happened:

- o **First five minutes:** Okay, this feels nice. I should do this more often.

- o **Next five minutes:** *Wait, did I leave the kitchen keys with my staff?*

- o **Another five minutes:** *What if my kids need me and I have my phone on silent?*

- o **By the end of the session:** Heart rate increased, stomach in knots, and full-blown **panic mode activated** because I had convinced myself something terrible had happened while I was lying there doing nothing.

And that, my friends, is how I managed to turn a relaxing massage into a near **existential crisis**.

Self-Care vs. Self-Sabotage: The Fine Line

The thing about anxious people is that we have **a talent for turning relaxation into guilt,** and guilt into stress, and stress into another excuse to avoid relaxing.

There are two types of self-care:

- o **The real, nourishing kind**—like eating a good meal, getting proper sleep, going for a walk, or journaling.

- o **The self-sabotaging kind**—where you convince yourself you're relaxing but are actually making things worse.

Here are some classic examples:

What You Think Is Self-Care	What It Actually Is
Taking a break from work	Checking emails while pretending to relax

Binge-watching a show to "de-stress"	Feeling guilty about wasting time the whole way through
Ordering comfort food	Eating too much, feeling bloated, then regretting it
Scrolling social media	Comparing yourself to strangers and feeling worse
Sleeping in to "catch up on rest"	Waking up late, feeling more tired, and panicking about wasted time

Attempt #3: The Forced Meditation Experiment

People always say, *"Just meditate, it'll calm your mind."* So, I tried.

I sat cross-legged on the floor, closed my eyes, and took a deep breath.

One second in: *Okay, focus on the breath.*

Three seconds in: *Did I pay that electricity bill?*

Five seconds in: *Wait, why is my heart beating so fast? Is this normal?*

Ten seconds in: *Should I be breathing slower? Faster? Am I doing this wrong?*

Eventually, I gave up, opened my eyes, and realized I had spent more time **overthinking meditation** than actually meditating.

Lesson learned? Meditation isn't for everyone—at least not *right away.* Sometimes, the best way to calm down is just to do something simple, like deep breathing or going for a short walk.

Hacks That Actually Work

If you're an anxious person who struggles with self-care, here are some **realistic** ways to make it work:

- **Set a Time Limit for "Relaxing"**

  o If you can't sit still for an hour, start with **five minutes**. Do something calming—drink tea, stretch, listen to music—without distractions.

- **Choose Active Relaxation**

  o Instead of forcing yourself to sit and do nothing (which is terrifying for an anxious mind), do something gentle—**gardening, painting, cooking, walking.**

- **The "One-Minute Rule"**

  o If something takes **less than a minute to do**, just do it immediately. It reduces mental clutter and prevents tasks from piling up.

- **Breathwork for Anxiety**

  o Try the **4-7-8 breathing technique**: Inhale for **4 seconds**, hold for **7 seconds**, and exhale for **8 seconds**. It's like hitting a reset button for your nervous system.

- **Create a "Worry Window"**

  o Set **10 minutes a day** to actively **worry about everything**. Once the time is up, move on. This tricks your brain into scheduling stress instead of letting it take over your whole day.

- **Do "Mini" Self-Care Instead of Big Plans**

  o Don't wait for a spa day or a vacation. Find **small moments of peace**—drink water, stretch for a minute, step outside, breathe deeply.

Final Thoughts: Learning to Truly Relax

Self-care is not a luxury; it's a **necessity**—especially when you're balancing work, kids, family, and your own mental health. But real self-care isn't about **expensive spa days or bubble baths**—it's about *doing what actually makes you feel good in the long run.*

For anxious people like us, the trick is **keeping it simple**. Instead of grand relaxation plans that stress us out even more, we just need **tiny, daily habits** that help us feel a little better, one moment at a time.

And if all else fails, just do what I do—**hug your kids, eat some fruit, take a deep breath, and remind yourself: "It's okay. I'm doing my best."** Because at the end of the day, that's the best kind of self-care there is.

Self-Care Beyond Spa Visits

(Or: Why Cleaning My Closet Feels Better Than a Bubble Bath)

Let's be real—when people hear *self-care*, they immediately picture scented candles, face masks, and a peaceful soak in a bathtub filled with overpriced bath salts. But honestly? Who has time for all that?

Between running a **vegan cloud kitchen**, raising two **high-energy kids**, taking **nutrition consultations**, and making sure my house doesn't collapse under a mountain of laundry, my version of self-care is **way less glamorous but far more satisfying**.

Because for people like us—the *always-busy, always-overthinking, always-doing-everything-for-everyone* types—self-care isn't about **relaxing**. It's about **taking back control**. And sometimes, that means **cleaning out the car, deleting 500 unread emails, or finally fixing that one drawer that never closes properly**.

The True Meaning of Self-Care (For Overwhelmed People Like Us)

Self-care is **anything that makes you feel better**, whether it's organizing your spice rack or finally **replying to the messages you've been ignoring for a month**.

Forget the **"aesthetic" self-care** Instagram tries to sell you. Instead, here are **realistic self-care ideas**—both for **busy**days (where you have 5 minutes) and **leisure** days (where you can actually breathe).

Self-Care for a Busy Day (a.k.a. Every Day of My Life)

Some days, there's **no time** for bubble baths or slow morning routines. On those days, self-care is about **tiny, effective actions** that make life *less chaotic*.

1. The "Two-Minute Rule" for Instant Relief

If something takes **less than two minutes**, do it immediately. No thinking, no procrastinating—just **get it done**.

- **Reply to that message.** (Stop overanalyzing it.)

- **Drink a glass of water.** (No, coffee doesn't count.)

- **Delete junk emails.** (Why do we still get emails from brands we bought one thing from 10 years ago?)

- **Put that one sock back in the drawer.** (How did it even end up in the kitchen?)

2. The Closet Purge Therapy

Some people do yoga to feel better. I **declutter my closet**.

There is something *deeply healing* about throwing out old clothes, especially the ones that:

- You *thought* you'd wear but never did.

- Are **"one size too small"** but you keep them *just in case*.

- Have been lying at the bottom of the drawer for **seven years**, waiting for their *big moment*.

The best part? **More space, less clutter, and zero guilt.**

3. The Car Clean-Up Mini Vacation

For some reason, **cleaning my car** makes me feel like I have my life together. Someone told me the state of your car is like the state of your mind-it reflects the clutter in your brain!

One minute, my car is **like an anxiety ridden brain** filled with empty bottles, old receipts, and a mystery snack wrapper from 2018. The next minute, I'm **Marie Kondo-ing the entire thing**, and suddenly—*bam!*—inner peace.

(Also, I finally find my lost lip balm. Win-win.)

4. The "Background Noise" Hack

Hate chores? Make them **entertaining**.

o **Folding laundry?** Play a podcast.

o **Cooking?** Watch a show.

o **Cleaning?** Blast music like you're in a Bollywood dance sequence.

Suddenly, boring tasks feel like **self-care instead of suffering**.

Self-Care for a Leisure Day (aka The Rarest Thing Ever)

On the rare occasion that you get a **lazy day**, here's how to make the most of it **without feeling guilty**.

1. The "Do Absolutely Nothing" Challenge

This is the hardest self-care practice ever: **sit down and do nothing**.

No phone. No emails. No *"let me just check one thing."* Just sit there, breathe, and let your brain chill for **at least 10 minutes**.

It will feel **uncomfortable** at first (because we are productivity addicts), but trust me—it's **worth it**.

2. The Lazy Luxury Routine

Self-care doesn't have to be *productive*. Sometimes, it's about **doing things just because they feel nice**.

- o **Oil your hair.** (Old-school but still the best.)

- o **Make a cup of herbal chai and actually enjoy it.** (Without scrolling.)

- o **Put on a face mask and pretend you're at a spa.**

3. The "No Plans" Day

Sometimes, self-care is saying **NO** to plans, expectations, and other people's needs.

Give yourself **one day** where you:

- Don't check emails.

- Don't cook (order in, guilt-free).

- Don't answer non-urgent calls.

Just exist. The world will survive without you (I promise).

Hacks for Everyday Self-Care

No matter how **busy or free you are**, these self-care **hacks** will make your life easier:

1. The "Night-Before" Rule

Mornings are **chaotic**. The secret? Prepare the night before.

- Choose your outfit before bed.

- Keep your bag, keys, and shoes ready at the door.

- Write down **the three most important tasks** for the next day.

Waking up without **morning panic** is the *real* self-care.

2. The "One Fun Thing" Rule

Every day, do **ONE small thing** that makes you happy:

- Eat something you love.

- Dance for five minutes.

- Call a friend just to **laugh**.

- Watch **satisfying cleaning videos** (we all do it).

3. The 5-4-3-2-1 Anxiety Trick

Feeling overwhelmed? Use this simple grounding technique:

- **5 things you see**

- **4 things you touch**

- **3 things you hear**

- **2 things you smell**

- **1 deep breath**

It instantly **calms** your mind.

4. The "Permission to Rest" Rule

Give yourself **permission to stop**.

Not every moment has to be **productive**. It's **okay** to rest, to sit quietly, to do something just for fun.

Self-care is about **balance**—and knowing when to push forward and when to pause.

Final Thoughts: Redefining Self-Care

Self-care isn't about **bubble baths and spa days** (unless you genuinely love them). It's about **doing whatever makes you feel sane and in control**—even if that means organising your pantry or finally **deleting that 2GB of photos forwards clogging your phone**.

So forget the idea that self-care has to look **a certain way**. If something makes **your** life easier, happier, or less stressful—even if it's as simple as **cleaning your desktop**—then guess what? **That's self-care.**

And if nothing else, just remember: **you can't pour from an empty cup**—so whatever fills *your* cup (even if it's just **a well-organised sock drawer**) is *totally valid.*

Journaling: My Brain Dump Strategy

If there's one thing that has saved my sanity (or whatever is left of it), it's journaling. No, really. If I had a rupee for every time journaling prevented me from texting something regrettable, stuffing my face with pani puri, or overthinking my entire existence—I'd probably own a wellness retreat by now.

But let's start at the beginning. I owe my introduction to this life-saving practice to **Rosemol Pinto** my former colleague at SHARAN and **Durgesh Nandini**. When they first suggested journaling, I was skeptical. "What will I write? Dear Diary, today my brain decided to overanalyze a stranger's tone at the grocery store?" But I gave it a shot, and turns out, journaling is less about writing poetic entries and more about dumping every single chaotic thought in your head onto paper—without judgment, without filters, and most importantly, without spell check.

Why Journaling is My Version of Therapy (Minus the Couch and Exorbitant Fees)

The thing about anxiety is that it's a noisy, messy, and utterly relentless companion. It's like that one relative who never stops talking and has an opinion on everything. The only way to deal with it? **Write it out.**

Journaling helps me:

- **Clear My Mental Clutter** – My brain on most days is like my car's glove compartment—filled with things I don't remember putting there. Thoughts pile up, anxieties layer themselves like a poorly made sandwich, and before I know it, I'm overwhelmed. Journaling helps me untangle the mess.

- **Stop the Mental Ping Pong** – One moment I'm worrying about my cloud kitchen orders, the next I'm wondering if my kids will remember to eat their fruits today, and before I know it, I'm debating if I should start a side hustle just in case all my existing projects collapse overnight. Writing it all down helps me spot what's actually worth worrying about and what's just my anxious brain inventing problems for fun.

- **Find Patterns in My Madness** – After journaling consistently, I started noticing trends. Like how my stress eating spikes before a big event, or how I always question my career choices around the same time every year. Journaling acts like a detective—it helps me see the "why" behind my reactions.

- **Prevent Texting Disasters** – You know those moments when you want to send an emotional, slightly dramatic text in the heat of the moment? Yeah, journaling is my intervention. I pour my feelings onto the page, and nine times out of ten, I realize an hour later that the text was unnecessary. Saved by the notebook!

- **Celebrate Small Wins** – Anxiety has a way of making you forget everything good that happens. My journal reminds me of the times I conquered my fears, handled situations better than expected, and—let's be real—resisted the urge to stress-eat an entire chocolate cake.

The Journaling Process: From Blank Page to Brain Dump

So how do I journal? Simple. **No rules. No grammar police. No judgment.** I don't start with a "Dear Diary" or poetic musings. Some days, my entries look like this:

"Why is my brain like this?"

«I'm tired. I need a break. But also, I need to work. WHY?"

"If I don't reply to a WhatsApp message within 2 minutes, will people think I'm ignoring them? WHY DO I CARE?"

And that's perfectly fine. Journaling isn't about being profound—it's about being **honest**.

Some Journaling Techniques That Work for Me

- **Brain Dump Journaling** – I literally write whatever is in my head, no structure, no coherence, just pure chaos on paper. Think of it as decluttering your mind the way you would clean out your closet.

- **Gratitude Journaling** – On especially anxious days, I force myself to list things I'm grateful for. Some days, it's deep (my kids, my health, my work). Other days, it's basic (the chai I had this morning was perfect, I found a parking spot easily). It helps shift my focus.

- **Future Self Letters** – When I'm feeling extra dramatic, I write letters to my future self. "Dear Future Me, if you're still stressing about the same thing in six months, please slap yourself with this notebook."

- **Question Journaling** – I ask myself questions like, "What's really bothering me?" or "Will this matter in a year?" The answers are often surprising.

What Journaling Has Revealed About Me

Journaling has been like therapy, but instead of a therapist nodding at me, I have my own words staring back. Some of the biggest realizations I've had:

o **I overthink 90% of things that don't need overthinking.**

o **My fears are often exaggerated and rarely come true.**

o **I'm way stronger than my anxious brain gives me credit for.**

o **My love for pani puri is directly proportional to my stress levels.**

o **My daughter is way more mature about food choices than I am.**

And the most important one?

o **I can be kinder to myself.**

Journaling: A Self-Love Practice (Not Just a Notebook Full of Rants)

If there's one thing I've learned, it's that journaling isn't about fixing myself. It's about **understanding myself**. Anxiety has been a part of my life for as long as I can remember, and instead of trying to fight it, I've learned to manage it—one journal entry at a time.

So, if you ever find yourself drowning in thoughts, unable to shut your brain up, or just feeling like you need an outlet that doesn't involve eating an entire tub of ice cream—**pick up a notebook and start writing.**

Your future self will thank you. And so will your sanity.

Movement for the Mind: Yoga, Walking, and Dance Therapy

If there's one thing that makes me feel like a normal, non-anxiety-ridden human being, it's movement. And no, I don't mean the frantic pacing I do when I'm overthinking a text I sent three hours ago. I mean intentional movement—the kind that calms my brain instead of sending it into overdrive.

Yoga, walking, and dance therapy are my go-to workouts, not just because they help me stay active, but because they somehow **switch off** the overthinking part of my brain. And let me tell you, **that's a miracle.**

Here's the funny part—I overthink everything in life. Every. Single. Thing. But when I do yoga, take a walk, or dance like nobody's watching (even when people **are** watching), I don't overthink a thing. I don't care if I look ridiculous, if my form is perfect, or if I'm doing it "right." It's **unfiltered me-time**, and it gives me a break from my own mind.

Why Movement Works for Anxiety (Like, Actually Works!)

Let's get a little science-y here. Anxiety is basically your body **stuck in fight-or-flight mode.** Your brain thinks there's a crisis (even when it's just a missed call from your kids), and it releases stress hormones like cortisol and adrenaline. Your heart races, your muscles tense up, and your breathing gets shallow.

Movement stops all that nonsense.

- o **Exercise increases blood flow to the brain** – More oxygen = clearer thoughts.

- o **It helps release endorphins** – Nature's happy hormones that act like natural anti-anxiety meds.

- o **It burns off excess adrenaline** – So your body realizes, "Hey, we're not being chased by a lion. Chill."

- o **It regulates breathing** – And we all know breathing like a human is key to surviving anxiety.

Yoga: The One Time I'm Not Overthinking Life

Now, I know yoga is supposed to be peaceful, but let me tell you, when I started, it was anything but.

First of all, **why are yoga instructors so calm?** I remember being in my first class, struggling to touch my toes, while the instructor gently said, "Listen to your breath." Ma'am, I can't hear my breath over the sound of my muscles screaming.

But then something magical happened. **I started focusing on my breath.** And for those few moments, my mind was quiet. No thoughts about work, no stress about my to-do list, no imaginary arguments playing out in my head. Just **me, my breath, and my wobbly attempt at balancing in tree pose.**

Over time, I realised that yoga was teaching me to **be present—** something anxiety absolutely hates. Anxiety thrives in the past and future. Yoga forces you to stay in the **now.**

Why Yoga is the Ultimate Anxiety Killer

- o **Breathing Control = Anxiety Control** – Deep breathing activates the parasympathetic nervous system, which tells your brain, "Calm down, it's all good."

- o **Slow Movements = Slow Thoughts** – Unlike cardio, yoga isn't about speed. It's about flow. And that flow translates to your mind.

- o **Stretching = Stress Relief** – Anxiety makes us tense. Yoga loosens us up—literally and mentally.

- o **You Can Do It Anywhere** – No gym membership, no fancy equipment, just a mat (or the floor, honestly).

I now do yoga in the morning, and it **sets the tone for my day.** Some days, I'm still overthinking after my session, but it's **less loud.** And that's a win.

Walking: My Therapy Sessions (With Myself)

Walking is **the most underrated anxiety fix.** It's simple, it's free, and it's effective. Plus, it's the **one workout where I don't even feel like I'm working out.**

I put on my sneakers, step outside, and suddenly, life doesn't feel like a disaster anymore. And if I add music or a podcast? **Even better.**

Walking helps me:

- o **Sort out my thoughts** (without spiraling)

- o **Get fresh air** (which is basically nature's way of saying, "Calm down")

- o **Move my body without effort** (low-impact but high-benefit)

- o **Escape my surroundings for a bit** (because sometimes, changing your location changes your mindset)

The Science Behind Why Walking Works

- o **Increases oxygen and blood flow to the brain** – More oxygen = better thinking, fewer irrational thoughts.

- o **Lowers cortisol levels** – The stress hormone goes down when you move.

- o **Releases pent-up tension** – Anxiety makes you feel stuck. Walking **unsticks** you.

Honestly, my best ideas come while walking. And so do my **biggest realisations**—like how overthinking never actually solves anything, but walking usually does.

Dance Therapy: My Favourite Form of Chaos

If walking is therapy and yoga is peace, **dancing is freedom.**

Nothing, and I mean **nothing**, makes me feel more alive than **blasting music and dancing like a crazy person.** And the best part? **I don't care how I look.**

- No judgment.

- No pressure.

- No thinking.

Just **movement and music.**

Why Dancing is the Ultimate Anxiety Antidote

- o **Cardio without the boring factor** – You're having fun while burning energy (and anxious thoughts).

- o **Increases dopamine and serotonin** – The brain chemicals responsible for happiness.

- o **Breaks the cycle of tension** – Anxiety makes your body stiff. Dancing makes it **loose and free.**

- o **Forces you to be in the moment** – Ever tried thinking about work stress while doing a full-on Bollywood thumka? Impossible.

For me, dancing is **pure joy.** It's where I feel completely uninhibited—something that anxiety usually doesn't let me be.

Why Movement is Key to Stopping an Anxiety Spiral

Anxiety spirals happen when our thoughts run wild and our body stays **still.** The best way to **interrupt** that? **Move.**

- • Feel an anxiety attack creeping up? **Walk.**

- • Mind racing at a million miles per hour? **Do yoga.**

- • Feeling like you're stuck in an anxious rut? **Blast music and dance.**

Movement shifts energy. It **forces your body to catch up with reality.**

Final Thoughts: Move to Make Your Mind Happy

I'm not saying movement will magically erase all anxiety (I wish), but I **am** saying that it's one of the few things that **instantly** makes me feel better.

So whether it's stretching on a yoga mat, walking around the block, or having a mini dance party in my kitchen, movement is my **secret weapon.**

And the best part? **No overthinking required.**

Chapter 5

The Social Struggle

Small Talk is My Personal Horror Film

You know those people who can just walk into a room, strike up a conversation with anyone, and leave with five new best friends? Yeah, I am *not* one of them.

For me, small talk is like being trapped in a **never-ending horror film** where I am the clueless victim, stumbling through awkward silences and overanalyzing everything I say.

o   **"Should I say 'Hi' first or let them notice me?"**

o   **"Did I introduce myself too fast? Did I sound weird?"**

o   **"Oh god, did I just interrupt them? Are they annoyed?"**

o   **"Now what do I say? Quick, think of something! WEATHER! Talk about the weather!"**

And the worst part? **I have to mentally rehearse** every conversation before it happens. I run through different scenarios like I'm preparing for an *exam*. What if they say this? What if they don't respond? What if they just walk away mid-sentence?!

Mimicking the Social Butterflies

I have watched in awe as my husband or SHARAN India's head Reyna glide through social gatherings with such **effortless charm**, striking up conversations as if it's the easiest thing in the world. Meanwhile, I am in the corner, clutching my drink like it's a life raft.

At this point, I'm convinced that some people are just **born knowing how to socialise**, while the rest of us are left reading "How to Talk to Humans" like it's a foreign language textbook.

So what do I do? **I mimic.**

I copy their confidence, their gestures, their small talk strategies. And for a few minutes, I can fool people into thinking I, too, am a functioning, social human being. That is, until the overthinking kicks in and I go back to nodding awkwardly.

Why is Small Talk So Hard for Anxious People?

Let's get a little scientific here. **Social anxiety** isn't just about shyness—it's a whole nervous system reaction.

- o **Fight-or-Flight Mode** – When faced with social situations, an anxious person's brain **registers it as a threat**. Your heart races, palms sweat, and your brain basically screams, **"RUN!"**

- o **Overactive Amygdala** – This is the fear center of your brain. For some people, it gets triggered by actual dangers (like a lion chasing them). For me, it gets triggered by the thought of making small talk at a networking event.

- o **Negative Self-Talk** – People with anxiety tend to **assume the worst** in social interactions. "What if they think I'm boring? What if they don't like me?"

- o **Mental Fatigue** – Overthinking **drains energy**, making socializing exhausting.

So if you struggle with small talk, it's not just you—it's literally **your brain chemistry working against you.**

Small Talk Hacks for the Socially Anxious

After years of dreading every networking event, wedding, and even casual grocery store interactions, I have **picked up a few survival hacks** that actually work.

1. The 3-Question Rule

Instead of panicking about what to say, follow this **golden rule: Ask three questions before talking about yourself.**

Example:

Me: *"So, how do you know the host?"*

Them: *"Oh, we went to college together."*

Me: *"Oh nice! Where did you study?"*

Them: *"Delhi University."*

Me: *"Great! What did you major in?"*

Boom. I've kept the conversation going for at least **30 seconds** without awkward silence.

Why does this work?

o **People love talking about themselves.**

o **It buys you time to think of your next sentence.**

o **It takes the pressure off you.**

2. Have a Few "Go-To" Small Talk Topics

I like to keep a **mental cheat sheet** of topics that work in almost every situation:

- Food – "Tried any good restaurants lately?"

- Travel – "Do you enjoy traveling? Any favourite places?"

- Movies/Shows – "What's the last thing you watched?"

- Pets – "Are you a dog or cat person?"

- Current Events (Nothing Controversial!) – "Did you hear about [funny/weird news story]?"

This way, I'm never stuck in that dreaded **"So…uh…nice weather?"** moment.

3. Use the FORD Technique

This is a popular conversation trick used by **actual** social people:

F – Family: "Do you have siblings?"

O – Occupation: "What do you do for work?"

R – Recreation: "What do you do for fun?"

D – Dreams: "Any exciting goals for this year?"

If you ever feel stuck in a conversation, just **pick a FORD topic**, and you'll have something to talk about.

4. The Compliment Opener (a lesson taken from my husband's handbook)

People love compliments. A great way to start a conversation is by giving a **genuine** compliment.

o   "I love your earrings! Where did you get them?"

o   "That colour looks amazing on you!"

o   "Your bag is so cool!"

Why does this work?

o   It **instantly makes the other person feel good.**

o   It opens up **an easy conversation path.**

(Just don't overdo it or sound creepy. Complimenting someone's shoes? Good. Complimenting their *eyelashes* in detail? Weird.)

5. Silence is NOT a Failure

One thing I've learned? **Awkward silences aren't actually that awkward.**

Sometimes, people just pause to think, sip their drink, or look around. **It's okay to let there be pauses.** You don't have to fill every second with words.

(Pro tip: If there's an awkward silence, **just smile.** It makes it seem intentional.)

Real-Life Struggles and Wins

Let me tell you about the time I tried **all of these tricks and still failed miserably.**

I was at a work event, and I thought, **"Okay, I got this."** I approached someone, gave them a compliment, and asked **the perfect first question.**

Me: *"So, what do you do for work?"*

Them: *"I'm a professional sleeper."*

Me: *"…Oh."*

I had no follow-up question. My brain just **froze.** Because how do you ask a **sleeper** about their job? *"Do you… sleep at work?"*

So yeah, **sometimes conversations flop.** But that's okay! **It happens to everyone.**

Final Thoughts: Small Talk Won't Kill You

Look, I'm never going to be the person who **effortlessly mingles** at a party. I will **always** have to psych myself up before making small talk.

But with a few tricks, I've gone from *completely avoiding conversations* to *being able to survive them without sweating through my shirt.*

So if small talk gives you anxiety, just remember:

o   **You're not alone.**

o   **Most people don't actually care if you're awkward.**

o   **There are hacks to make it easier.**

And worst case? Just mimic the nearest confident person and hope for the best. **It works.**

Creating Your Tribe: Finding People Who Get It

There was a time when I thought that having **a million friends** was the ultimate goal. You know, the Bollywood fantasy where you have a *huge* gang, always laughing, always hanging out, basically living in a Karan Johar movie.

Spoiler alert: **That's not real life.**

Real life is when you have **three or four solid people** who won't judge you when you say, *"I need a minute."* Who understand when your anxiety kicks in, who don't make you feel guilty when you cancel plans (again), and who will **answer your call at 2 AM** without questioning your life choices.

The Myth of the Giant Friend Circle

At one point in life, I collected people like **Diwali sweets**—hoarding friendships, trying to please everyone, thinking that the more people I had, the **less lonely I'd be.**

Reality check? **That did not work.**

Because when you have **too many people around**, you're constantly **adapting**, trying to keep up with everyone's expectations, never really being yourself.

I remember going out with **a big group** once, trying to enjoy, but internally:

o   **Why am I here?**

o   **Why is this conversation so forced?**

o   **Can I go home now?**

o   **If I leave early, will they talk about me?**

And so, I sat there, **pretending to be interested**, while all I wanted was **to be in bed, eating a big bowl of fruit with my book.**

That's when I realized: **quality over quantity.**

The 3-4 People Who Actually Get You

You know what's better than **twenty half-hearted friendships?**

Three or four rock-solid ones.

These are the people who:

o   **Don't judge you** when you say, *"I'm too drained to socialize today."*

o   **Understand your anxiety** and don't make you feel guilty about it.

o   **Check in on you** even when you disappear for a while.

o   **Stand by you** when you need to rant, cry, or just stare into space.

And I'm **blessed** to have these people. (Hello Kripa, Amol, Bijal, Shra Tai) No matter how chaotic my life gets—with work, my cloud kitchen, my family, my consultations—there are a **few people** who will always return my call or just send a *"Hey, you okay?"* text.

Sometimes, **that's all you need.**

Some People Come, Some People Go (And It Hurts, But It's Okay)

Now, let's talk about the **painful** part.

I've had people come into my life, **guide me, support me, show me the way**—and then? They left.

And I **overthought their exit** like it was a movie scene that needed analyzing.

o   *Did I do something wrong?*

o   *Was I not good enough?*

o   *Should I have done more to keep them in my life?*

Turns out, **not everyone is meant to stay forever.**

Some people come into your life **for a purpose**—to **teach you something, to help you through a phase, to be there when you need them the most.** And when their role is over, they move on.

And you know what? **That's okay.**

At first, it *doesn't* feel okay. It feels **like a breakup**—except you don't even get closure.

But looking back, I see that **every person who left** played a role in shaping me. Some taught me **kindness**, some taught me **strength**, some taught me **what not to tolerate.**

So now, instead of **clinging onto the loss**, I just say, *"Thank you for your time in my life."*

(And then I still overthink it for at least three months, but hey, progress.)

Setting Boundaries (Or: How I Stopped Being a People-Pleasing Mess)

Once upon a time, I had **no boundaries.**

If someone needed something, I said yes.

If someone wanted my time, I said yes.

If someone crossed a line, I still said yes.

Because saying no felt **mean**, and I didn't want to disappoint people.

Big mistake

I ended up drained, anxious, and mentally **exhausted** because I was constantly putting **other people's needs above my own.**

It took me **years** to realize: *"Wait… I can say no???"*

Now? I protect my energy like it's **a plate of pani puri in a room full of hungry people.**

Signs That You Need to Set Boundaries:

o   You feel **resentful** after saying yes to something.

o   You feel **drained** after spending time with certain people.

o   You say yes **out of guilt**, not because you actually want to.

o   You feel like you're constantly **giving, but not receiving.**

So, I started **setting boundaries**, and honestly? Best decision ever.

- o **No, I can't take this call right now.**

- o **No, I don't have the bandwidth for this.**

- o **No, I'm not comfortable with this conversation.**

And guess what? The right people **respected my boundaries.**

The wrong people? **Got offended and left.** (*Which just proved that they weren't meant to be in my life anyway.*)

Toxic Family? Distance Is Your Best Friend

Now, let's address the **elephant in the room—family.**

We're told: *"Family is everything."*

But let's be real—**not all family members are healthy for us.**

Some are **judgmental.**

Some are **manipulative.**

Some are **toxic in ways we don't even realize until later.**

And cutting off a toxic family member? **Oh, the guilt!** Society makes you feel like you're committing a crime.

But here's what I've learned:

Your **mental peace** is more important than **any imposed obligation.**

You do not owe anyone your energy just because they're "family."

- o If they drain you, **step back.**

- o If they disrespect you, **set boundaries.**

- o If they cause **more harm than good, distance yourself.**

Minimal contact. **No guilt.**

(*Okay, maybe a little guilt at first, but trust me, it fades.*)

How to Find Your Tribe (If You Haven't Yet)

If you're still in the process of **finding your tribe**, here's some advice:

o   **Don't force it.** You can't just **pick random people** and expect them to be your ride-or-die tribe. The right people will come into your life naturally.

o   **Pay attention to how you feel around them.** If you feel like you have to **pretend** or **overthink** everything you say, they're probably not tribe material.

o   **Look for people who listen.** Your tribe should consist of people who **truly listen** to you, not just wait for their turn to talk.

o   **Test the waters with boundaries.** Set small boundaries and see how they react. If they respect them, you might have found a keeper.

And remember, your tribe doesn't have to be big. It's not about quantity; it's about **quality**. Even if you have just **one**person who truly gets you, that's enough.

The Importance of Letting Go

Lastly, let's talk about something that took me a while to learn—**letting go**.

As much as we want to **hold on to everyone** who crosses our path, not everyone is meant to stay. Some people are just there to teach you a lesson, guide you for a little while, or even help you discover something about yourself.

And when they leave? It's okay. It's part of the journey.

It's natural to feel **hurt** when someone you cared about leaves your life. It's natural to **overthink** their departure. But with time, you'll realize that their role in your life was complete.

And now, you're free to focus on the people who are **meant to stay—** your tribe.

Final Thoughts

Building your tribe takes time, patience, and a lot of self-reflection. You'll have to set boundaries, let go of toxic people, and maybe even say goodbye to those who were only meant to be in your life for a season.

But when you finally have that small, tight-knit group of people who truly get you? **It's worth all the overthinking, the heartache, and the lessons learned along the way.**

So, here's to your tribe—the people who make life **a little less overwhelming** and remind you that you're not alone on this journey. And if you haven't found them yet, don't worry. They're out there, and when the time is right, they'll find you too.

Chapter 6
Developing Coping Mechanisms

Rewiring Thought Patterns: Cognitive Hacks That Keep Me (Mostly) Sane

If I had a mango for every time someone told me, *"Just think positive!"* when I was spiraling into an anxiety-fueled overthinking marathon, I'd probably be running a full-fledged mango orchard instead of writing this chapter. Because let's be real—**rewiring thought patterns is not as easy as flipping a switch.**

If my brain were a computer, it would have at least **437 open tabs**, a bunch of background apps draining my battery, and a pop-up ad screaming *"YOU FORGOT TO PAY YOUR BILLS!"* every five minutes. And unlike actual computers, there's no simple "clear cache" button for anxiety. **But there are hacks.** Cognitive hacks that help me **calm the storm, stop overthinking, and prevent myself from jumping to wild conclusions** like *"That person didn't reply, which means they secretly hate me, and I should probably change my name and move to a different city."*

So, let me share some of the funniest, most ridiculous, and surprisingly effective cognitive tricks I've developed over the years.

1. The "What Would My Husband Say?" Trick

Now, my husband is one of those people who can walk into a room full of strangers, **charm them effortlessly**, and leave with five new best friends. Meanwhile, I'm the person standing in the corner trying to figure out if I can escape without being noticed.

But what I admire most about him is his **cool-headed, rational approach to life**. Where I see **potential disaster**, he sees **mild inconvenience**. Where I imagine **worst-case scenarios**, he assumes *"It'll work out somehow."*

So, when my brain starts **catastrophizing** a situation, I pause and think:

"What would my husband say about this?"

Example:

- o   **Me:** "Oh my god, I made a typo in that email to my client. They're going to think I'm an idiot and never work with me again."

- o   **Imaginary Husband in My Head:** "Or they won't even notice. And if they do, they'll move on with their lives in five seconds."

It sounds silly, but this little trick **snaps me out of overthinking mode**. Sometimes, all we need is to borrow **someone else's rationality** when our own is malfunctioning.

2. The "Will This Matter in 5 Days?" Rule

I once spent **three hours** agonizing over whether I came across as rude in a conversation. **THREE HOURS.** Over a conversation that said, *"Hey, can't make it today. Let's reschedule?"*

Three days later, I couldn't even remember why I was stressed about it.

So, now I use the **"Will this matter in 5 days?" rule.** If something is causing me to spiral, I ask myself:

o   **Will I remember this in five days?**

o   **Will this actually affect my life long-term?**

o   **Is this worth losing my peace over?**

99% of the time, the answer is *NO*. And if it's not going to matter in five days, it **definitely** shouldn't be stealing my energy today.

3. The "Ridiculous Worst-Case Scenario" Method

Anxiety loves to **make up terrible stories**.

o   *"You're going to mess up your presentation and get bad reviews"*

o   *"That client hasn't responded, which means they're mad at you."*

o   *"Your friend hasn't texted back in three hours. She must be secretly plotting your downfall."*

Now, instead of letting these thoughts spiral, I **one-up my anxiety** by making the **worst-case scenario even more ridiculous**.

Example:

o   **Original Anxiety Thought:** "What if I say something stupid during my Zoom workshop?"

o   **Me:** "Oh no! And then they'll cancel all my future sessions! And then my career will end! And I'll have to move to a remote village and become a coconut farmer!"

By exaggerating the worst-case scenario to **absurd** levels, I force myself to **see how ridiculous my fears are**. Suddenly, the original thought loses its power.

4. The "You're Not That Important" Reality Check

This one might sound harsh, but hear me out.

One of my biggest anxiety triggers used to be **what other people thought of me**. Did I say the wrong thing? Did I sound stupid? Did I accidentally offend someone?

Then I had an **epiphany**:

Nobody is thinking about me as much as I think they are.

People are **too busy worrying about their own lives** to be analyzing my every move.

Once I realized this, life became **so much easier**. Now, when I start overanalyzing an interaction, I remind myself:

"They probably forgot about this five minutes after it happened."

And suddenly, the weight of the moment disappears.

5. The "Do the Opposite" Strategy

My anxious brain tells me to **avoid** situations that make me uncomfortable. So, naturally, one of the most powerful hacks is to **do the exact opposite.**

Example:

- o   My brain says, *"Cancel that event, you're too nervous."* → I go anyway.

- o   My brain says, *«Don't send that message, you'll sound dumb."* → I send it.

- o   My brain says, *"You should avoid confrontation forever."* → I speak up.

Every time I **override** my anxiety by doing the opposite of what it wants, I **weaken its grip** on me. It doesn't always go perfectly, but at least I don't let fear dictate my life.

6. The "Talk to Yourself Like You Would a Friend" Trick

If a friend came to me and said, *"I'm freaking out because I sent a message with a typo,"* I'd laugh and tell them, *"Nobody cares about typos. You're fine!"*

But when I make a typo? Oh, suddenly it's a **national crisis.**

Why are we so much **harsher** on ourselves than we are on others?

So, now I try to **talk to myself the way I would talk to a friend.** Whenever my brain is being **mean**, I pause and ask:

"If my best friend told me this, what would I say to her?"

And then, I say that **to myself.**

7. The "Worst First, Then Fun" Rule

Sometimes, anxiety is just about **avoiding things we don't want to do.** Procrastination, perfectionism, and avoidance—**they're all anxiety's best friends.**

So, I use the **"Worst First, Then Fun"** rule.

o   Hate sending emails? Do it first.

o   Dreading a difficult conversation? Get it over with.

o   Stressed about a work task? Start it immediately.

Once the **worst** thing is done, my anxiety **instantly reduces**, and I actually enjoy the rest of my day.

Final Thoughts: Small Steps, Big Changes

Rewiring thought patterns isn't about **suddenly becoming a zen master** overnight. It's about making **small, consistent changes** that help you handle life with **less stress and more ease.**

So, whether it's using the **"Will this matter in 5 days?"** trick, exaggerating worst-case scenarios, or reminding yourself that **nobody is**

analyzing your every move, these little cognitive hacks can make a **huge** difference.

And trust me, if someone like me—who overanalyzes WhatsApp messages and has **entire debates with imaginary people in my head**— can learn to rewire her thoughts, **so can you**

Meditation for People Who Can't Sit Still

(Or: How I Finally Stopped Treating My Brain Like a Chaotic WhatsApp Group)

If there were a **Nobel Prize for Overthinking**, I'd have won it multiple times by now. My brain is like a **Google Chrome browser with 87 tabs open, and at least 5 of them are frozen, but I refuse to restart the computer**. The idea of sitting still and *not doing anything*? **That felt unnatural, borderline illegal.**

But meditation? Oh, I had heard about it. It was like that **mysterious skincare routine that people swear by but I never quite figured out**. You know the type—calm, glowing people who sip herbal tea and effortlessly radiate peace. Meanwhile, I was the person who, if asked to sit still for five minutes, would start planning dinner, checking my phone, and mentally drafting an email—all at once.

However, over the years, **I've cracked the meditation code**. I still can't sit cross-legged for hours like a Himalayan monk, but I've worked my way up to **7–10 minutes of real, focused meditation**. And let me tell you, it has done wonders for my anxious brain.

If you, like me, find the idea of sitting quietly and doing *nothing* completely unnatural, **welcome to the club!** Let's talk about why meditation is hard for us overthinkers, how I went from an absolute beginner to a (semi) regular meditator, and some **hilarious but effective tricks to get your mind to shut up**—even if it's just for a few minutes.

Why Meditation Feels Impossible for Overthinkers

- **Your brain doesn't have an "off" switch**

  - You sit down to meditate, and suddenly your brain decides to remember *every embarrassing thing you've ever done since childhood.*

- **Breath? What breath?**

  - The moment you try to focus on breathing, your brain goes: *Are we breathing too fast? Too slow? What if I forget how to breathe?*

- **Restlessness kicks in**

  - After exactly **47 seconds**, you start feeling an urge to move, check your phone, adjust your posture, or scratch an itch that didn't exist before you started meditating.

- **Expectation vs. Reality is hilarious**

  - *Expectation:* Sitting peacefully like Buddha, radiating calm.

  - Reality: Checking how much time is left, wondering why your leg is asleep, and questioning all your life choices.

How I Finally Got into Meditation (Without Losing My Mind)

I realized that expecting myself to **sit still in absolute silence** was a recipe for failure. So, I started **cheating my way in**—and guess what? **It worked!**

1. Guided Meditation: The Training Wheels

At first, I needed **someone else to tell me what to do** because my brain was too stubborn to listen to me. I started with short, **5-minute guided meditations** where someone's soothing voice would remind me to focus on my breath instead of my grocery list.

2. The "Moving Meditation" Trick

If you think meditation means **sitting in one place**, let me tell you—**walking can be meditation too**. I found that a slow, mindful walk, where I simply focused on the sensation of my feet hitting the ground, was **way easier** than sitting in stillness.

3. Counting Breaths (Because My Brain Likes Numbers)

Since my mind always needs *something* to do, I started **counting my breaths**—inhale (1), exhale (2), inhale (3)… If I lost track (which happened often), I just started over. **No pressure, no overthinking.**

4. The "One-Minute Rule" That Changed Everything

I tricked my anxious mind by saying, **"You only have to meditate for one minute."** One minute feels like nothing! But the funny thing is, once I sat down for a minute, I would often go longer **because the hardest part was just starting**.

5. Mantras for the Overthinker

Sometimes, focusing on breath alone felt impossible, so I used **mantras**—simple phrases I repeated in my head like:

o *I am calm, I am safe, I am present.*

o *This moment is enough.*

o *Nothing is urgent right now.*

This helped drown out my usual mental noise (e.g., *Did I reply to that email? Why did I say that stupid thing in 2009?*).

6. Using a Meditation Ritual

To make meditation feel **less like a chore**, I created a small **ritual around it**. I light a candle or use essential oils, which makes the practice feel more **special and enjoyable**.

7. Accepting That Some Days Will Be a Disaster

Some days, I can meditate for **10 whole minutes** without much effort. Other days, **my brain is a stubborn toddler throwing a tantrum**. And that's okay! Meditation is about *practicing*, not *perfecting*.

Funny Meditation Fails (That You'll Relate To)

- **The Meditation-Nap Confusion**

  - There have been days when I sat down to meditate and woke up 20 minutes later. Apparently, **my body decided a nap was more important than enlightenment.**

- **The Intrusive Thought Festival**

  - Me: *Okay, let's focus on the breath.*

  - My Brain: *Remember that weird dress you bought five years ago and never wore it? Let's think about it for the next 10 minutes!*

- **The "Wait, Is This Meditation or Just Sitting?" Dilemma**

  - There have been times when I just stared at a wall, and I honestly don't know if I was meditating or just zoning out. **Either way, it was peaceful.**

Easy Meditation Hacks for Restless People

- **Start Small** – Even **one minute counts.** Build up slowly.

- **Use Music** – Calm, instrumental music can help keep your mind from wandering.

- **Try Body Scanning** – Instead of focusing only on breath, mentally scan your body from head to toe, noticing any tension.

- **Use a Meditation App** – There are great apps like Insight Timer, Calm, or Headspace that guide you.

- **Meditate at the Same Time Daily** – Helps build a habit. Morning or bedtime works best.

- **Let Go of Perfection** – Even a "bad" meditation session is better than none.

- **Laugh at Yourself** – Because sometimes, meditation is just sitting there thinking about how bad you are at meditation. And that's okay!

The Magic of Meditation: What Changed for Me

o **Less Anxiety Freakouts** – I still have them, but I bounce back **faster**.

o **Better Focus** – My brain isn't *always* in five places at once now.

o **More Patience** – Especially with my kids, work, and (let's be honest) *my husband's intermittent fasting talks.*

o **Feeling More in Control** – Instead of **reacting** to anxiety, I can **pause and respond** better.

Final Thoughts: Meditation Is for YOU, Too!

If you think you *can't* meditate, trust me—I was the same. But **starting small, making it fun, and accepting imperfection** made all the difference. You don't need to be a spiritual guru. You just need to **breathe, sit for a bit, and not take it too seriously.**

And if all else fails? **There's always walking meditation.** Because let's be real—**sitting still is overrated.**

Grounding Techniques That Actually Work

(Or: How to Stop Your Brain from Running a Marathon Without Your Permission)

You know those moments when your mind **goes into overdrive**, your heart races like you're being chased by a wild animal (but really, it's just an email notification), and suddenly you're questioning every life decision you've ever made?

Yep, welcome to **anxiety-ville**. Population: Us.

For the longest time, my coping mechanism was **panic, followed by overthinking, followed by regretting the overthinking**. But then I discovered **grounding techniques**, and let me tell you—they're **like pressing the reset button on a glitchy laptop (a.k.a. my brain)**.

So, if you're tired of anxiety turning your mind into a chaotic WhatsApp group where every thought is shouting at once, **let's talk about grounding**—what it is, how it works, and, most importantly, how to do it in a way that actually makes sense for us overthinkers.

What Is Grounding? (And Why Should You Care?)

Grounding is **basically the art of getting out of your head and back into reality**. It's like telling your anxious brain, **"Hey, stop time-traveling into the past and future. Let's focus on *right now*."**

It works by using your **senses, movement, or mental exercises** to bring you back to the present moment. And the best part? **It actually works.**

So, let's jump into some of my favorite **tried-and-tested grounding techniques**—ones that don't require an expensive meditation retreat or a PhD in mindfulness.

1. The 5-4-3-2-1 Method (a.k.a. The Anxiety Emergency Exit Plan)

This is my go-to technique when I feel like my brain is about to launch into **full-blown chaos mode**. It's simple, effective, and works almost instantly.

How It Works:

You use your **five senses** to reconnect with the present moment.

- **5 things you can see** – *The chair, the window, the random sock on the floor…*

- **4 things you can touch** – *Your phone, your hair, the smooth surface of the table…*

- **3 things you can hear** – *The hum of the fan, distant traffic, your own breathing…*

- **2 things you can smell** – *Coffee, the shampoo in your hair (or, let's be real, your kid's leftover snacks in the car)…*

- **1 thing you can taste** – *Chew gum, sip tea, or just notice the lingering taste of your last meal.*

Why It Works:

Your brain can't spiral into *What if this happens?* and *I should have said that!* when it's busy identifying objects around you. **It forces you to focus on reality instead of your anxiety's horror movie.**

My Funny Experience with This:

Once, I was mid-panic attack in my kitchen and started doing this exercise. When I got to **things I could smell**, the only thing I could register was **burnt toast** because I had completely forgotten I was making breakfast. So, technically, **this exercise not only grounded me but also saved my toaster.**

2. "Name It to Tame It" (Because Brains Hate Vague Fears)

Sometimes, anxiety feels like **a giant dark cloud hovering over your head**, but you don't even know what it's about. That's where this technique comes in.

How It Works:

Literally **say out loud** (or write down) what's making you anxious.

Example:

o   *"I feel anxious because I have a work deadline tomorrow."*

o   *"I'm stressed because I need to call the doctor and I hate making phone calls."*

o   *"I'm overwhelmed because my to-do list looks like a grocery receipt."*

Why It Works:

Your brain thrives on **vagueness** when it comes to anxiety. The moment you **identify the exact fear**, it stops feeling like a monster in the shadows and more like **a problem you can actually deal with.**

My Funny Experience with This:

One day, I was feeling anxious but didn't know why. I sat down and wrote: *"I feel weird because… I don't know why."* Then I thought harder and realized it was because I had **forgotten to drink Green Smoothie that morning.** Turns out, I wasn't actually having an existential crisis—I was just **nutrient deprived.**

3. The "Cold Shock" Trick (a.k.a. Anxiety's Kryptonite)

When my brain is in **full freak-out mode**, I need something **fast** to snap me out of it. That's when I use the **cold water trick.**

How It Works:

o   Splash **cold water** on your face.

o   Hold an **ice cube** in your hand.

o   Take a **cold shower** if things feel really bad.

Why It Works:

Cold temperatures **activate your vagus nerve**, which calms your nervous system almost immediately. It's like your body's built-in "chill pill."

My Funny Experience with This:

Once, I was trying to calm myself down before a SHARAN workshop, so I held an ice cube… and **promptly dropped it because it was too cold.** Ended up spending the next two minutes **chasing it across the kitchen floor**—which, ironically, completely distracted me from my anxiety.

4. The "Brain Dump" Method (Because Overthinkers Need an Outlet)

If your anxiety **feels like 100 browser tabs open in your head**, sometimes you just need to **dump all those thoughts onto paper**.

How It Works:

o   Grab a notebook (or open the Notes app).

o   Write **everything** that's bothering you—**no filter, no grammar check, no logic needed.**

o   Once it's out of your head, you'll feel **lighter and clearer.**

Why It Works:

Your brain is **not a storage unit.** If you're holding on to 100 different worries at once, your anxiety will keep **hitting refresh on them all day.** Writing them down **declutters your mind** so it can finally breathe.

My Funny Experience with This:

I once wrote an entire **five-page rant** about how much I hate waiting on hold for customer service. By the end, I wasn't even anxious anymore—I was just **laughing at my own unnecessary drama.**

5. Movement (Because Anxiety Hates Exercise)

If your mind is running in circles, **make your body do the same.**

How It Works:

- o   Take a **short walk** (even if it's just around your living room).

- o   Do **jumping jacks** or dance like nobody's watching.

- o   Stretch your arms and legs **as if you're a sleepy cat.**

Why It Works:

Anxiety is just **a bunch of nervous energy with nowhere to go**. Moving your body **burns some of that energy** so your brain can stop overloading.

My Funny Experience with This:

One time, I got so anxious before a big meeting that I started **jumping around my room like a kangaroo.** My daughter walked in, gave me a look, and said, **"Are you okay, or are we getting a pet rabbit?"**

Final Thoughts: Grounding = Anxiety's Worst Nightmare

Anxiety **loves keeping you trapped in your own head.** Grounding techniques **pull you out of that spiral and bring you back to reality—** where, more often than not, things aren't as catastrophic as they seem.

Try these out and **see which ones work best for you.** And remember— **it's okay to have anxious days.** The goal isn't to be anxiety-free all the time (if only!). The goal is to have **tools that help you deal with it without losing your mind.**

And if all else fails? **Try chasing an ice cube across the floor.** Trust me, it works.

The Power of Saying "No" Without Guilt

(Or: How I Stopped Being a People-Pleasing Doormat and Finally Took My Life Back)

Let's start with a confession: **I used to be completely incapable of saying "no."**

And I don't mean the *"Oh, I guess I'll help out even though I don't want to"* kind of thing. No, I mean the **full-blown, self-sacrificing, what-was-I-thinking level of YES-ing everything to my own detriment.**

I've said yes to **work projects I had no time for**, yes to **helping people move houses when I could barely move my own furniture**, yes to **events I didn't want to attend**, yes to **last-minute favors that made me want to scream**, and even yes to **eating food I despised just because I didn't want to offend anyone.**

Saying no used to feel like I was **committing a crime**—like I'd personally ruined someone's day just by declining an invitation. The guilt would eat me up inside, and before I knew it, I'd be stuck in situations that made me **want to throw myself into a vat of hot chai.**

But guess what? I finally **cracked the code** on how to say no **without guilt** (well, 80% of the time—let's be realistic), and let me tell you, it has **saved my sanity.**

So, if you're like past-me, constantly drowning in **commitments you don't actually want to be part of**, let's fix that. **Right now.**

Why Is Saying "No" So Hard?

For most of us, saying "no" isn't hard because we *actually* want to say yes. It's hard because of **three things:**

o **We don't want to disappoint people.** (*"What if they get mad? What if they think I'm rude?"*)

o **We feel obligated.** (*"I mean… I should help them, right?"*)

o **We don't know how to say no without sounding mean.** (*"Can I say no without sounding like a heartless villain?"*)

And if you're a recovering people-pleaser like me, these thoughts make **every "no" feel like a personal attack on someone's soul.**

But here's the thing: **Saying no is not rude. It's not selfish. It's survival.**

And honestly, **nobody is out here handing out awards for Most Self-Sacrificing Human.**

So let's dive into the **hacks that helped me stop overcommitting and start protecting my peace**—without feeling like an evil mastermind.

1. The Magic of "No, But…"

One of my biggest fears about saying no was that it would make me seem **cold or unhelpful.** But then I learned the power of **"No, but…"**

How It Works:

You say no **without actually shutting the door completely.**

Instead of:

■ *"No, I can't help you."* (*which feels blunt and harsh*) Say:

■ *"I can't help today, but I'd be happy to send you some useful resources!"*

- *"I can't take on this extra work, but I can help brainstorm some solutions."*

- *"I won't be able to attend, but I'd love to catch up another time."*

Why It Works:

This makes it **easier to say no without guilt** because you're **still offering some kind of support**—just **on your own terms**.

Real-Life Example:

A friend once asked me to help her **plan a surprise party.** I knew if I said yes, I'd end up doing **all the heavy lifting** while she just showed up looking fabulous. (**Been there, done that, never again.**)

So instead of saying **"No, I'm too busy"**, I said:

"I can't plan the whole thing, but I'd love to help with ideas! Maybe I can send you some cool themes and vendors?"

She was thrilled, I **avoided being trapped in a three-month planning nightmare**, and **everyone was happy.**

2. The "Delay and Deflect" Method

If you're someone who **panics under pressure** and says yes before even thinking, this trick is a lifesaver.

How It Works:

Instead of **immediately saying yes, buy yourself time** to decide.

Say things like:

- *"Let me check my schedule and get back to you."*

- *"I need to think about it—can I let you know later today?"*

- *"I have a lot going on right now—can I confirm tomorrow?"*

Why It Works:

- o It **removes the pressure** of making a decision on the spot.

- o It **gives you time** to decide if you actually want to do it.

- o It makes **saying no later feel easier.**

Real-Life Example:

A relative once called and said, **"Can you host the entire family for dinner this Sunday?" (Mind you, this was on a Friday.)**

Past me would have **panicked and agreed immediately.**

But new me? I calmly said:

"Let me check my weekend schedule and I'll get back to you!"

Two hours later, I texted:

"Hey! I checked, and I'm actually tied up this weekend. Maybe we can plan for another time?"

No stress. No overthinking. No last-minute cooking disasters.

3. The "Broken Record" Trick (For When People Just Won't Take No for an Answer)

Some people just **won't accept your no** and will keep **pushing, guilt-tripping, or trying to convince you.**

For them, you need the **broken record** technique.

How It Works:

You **repeat your no in different ways until they get the message.**

Example:

- **Them:** "Come on, it's just one small favor!"

- **You:** "I really can't. I have too much on my plate."

- **Them:** "But it won't take much time!"

- **You:** "I totally understand, but I'm really not available."

- **Them:** "You're being so difficult!"

- **You:** "I hear you, but my answer is still no."

Why It Works:

o **It stops people from wearing you down.**

o **It shuts down guilt-tripping.**

o **It reinforces your boundary without escalating conflict.**

Real-Life Example:

A colleague once **kept pushing me to join a project** I had **zero interest in.** After declining politely twice, she **still wouldn't let it go.**

So I kept repeating: *"I wish I could help, but I really can't take this on right now."*

After the **fourth repeat**, she gave up. (**Victory!**)

4. Accept That "No" Is a Full Sentence

I used to feel like I needed to **justify every no with a 500-word essay.** But the truth is:

- *"I can't."*

- *"That won't work for me."*

- *"I'm not available."*

Are all perfectly acceptable answers.

You don't owe people **a detailed explanation** every time you say no.

Real-Life Example:

A friend once asked me, **"Can you bake 100 cupcakes for my kid's school event?"**

Past me: *"Well, I have a lot of work, but maybe if I stay up all night I can manage…"*

New me: *"Oh, I can't, but I hope you find someone to help!"* (**And then I changed the topic.**)

Final Thoughts: Protect Your Time Like a Boss

Saying no is one of the **most powerful self-care tools** you can have. It doesn't mean you're selfish. It doesn't mean you don't care.

It just means you **value your time, energy, and mental peace.**

So start practicing these **hacks**, and watch your life transform. **Trust me, you'll never go back to the old yes-everything version of you.**

Chapter 7

Becoming Self-Reliant

Learning to Be Your Own Safe Space

(Or: How to Be Your Own Best Friend Without Waiting for a Rescue Mission)

Let's be honest—**waiting for someone else to save you is like waiting for a WiFi signal in the middle of a jungle.**

Not happening.

For the longest time, I believed that **my safe space** was **other people—** my family, my friends, my mentors, my therapist, even my houseplants (yes, I used to have full conversations with my aloe vera).

I thought **if I surrounded myself with the right people, the right environment, and enough distractions, I'd feel secure.**

Spoiler alert: **That didn't happen.**

Why? Because the **most important safe space isn't external.** It's **internal.** It's **you.**

You can have the best support system in the world, but if you don't have **your own back,** if you don't **believe in yourself, cheer for yourself, and pick yourself up when life smacks you down,** then all the outside help in the world **won't be enough.**

So let's talk about how to **become your own safe space**—your **own biggest supporter, your own rescue team, and your own best friend.**

Step 1: Love Yourself More Than Anyone Else (Yes, Really)

Now, I know what you're thinking:

„Umm… isn't that selfish?"

Nope. **Not even a little.**

Loving yourself **more than anyone else** doesn't mean you stop caring about people. It means **you stop abandoning yourself** in the process of caring for others.

For years, I'd bend over backward for people—even when I was exhausted, overworked, or completely drained.

o   I said yes when I wanted to say no.

o   I took on responsibilities that weren't mine.

o   I ignored my own needs just to make others comfortable.

And guess what? **Nobody gave me a medal for it.** Not a single award ceremony in my honor. Just **burnout, stress, and the occasional stress-induced breakout.**

Then one day, I had an **epiphany:**

"If I don't take care of myself, who will?"

So, I started doing **small things to show myself love:**

- Saying no when I meant no.

- Taking breaks without guilt.

- Feeding myself properly instead of running on coffee.

- Speaking to myself kindly instead of like a drill sergeant.

And the craziest thing happened—**life didn't fall apart.**

In fact, it got **better.** Because when you love yourself, you attract **better people, better opportunities, and a whole lot of peace.**

Step 2: Be Your Own Best Friend (Because Who Else Will Be There 24/7?)

Ever noticed how **we're so kind to our friends** but **so harsh on ourselves?**

If a friend fails at something, we say:

"It's okay, you'll get it next time!"

But if **we** fail?

"Wow, I'm such an idiot. I can't do anything right."

Excuse me, **WHAT?**

If you wouldn't say it to your best friend, **don't say it to yourself.**

Being your own best friend means:

- **Encouraging yourself when things go wrong.**

  "Okay, that sucked, but we're learning. Next time, we'll do better."

- **Treating yourself with kindness.**

  "You're doing your best. That's enough."

- **Celebrating your wins—even the small ones.**

  "You woke up on time today? WIN. You made it through a stressful day without losing your mind? WIN."

Real-Life Example:

There was a time when I completely **messed up a live cooking demo.**

o   I forgot ingredients.

o   I knocked over a blender.

o   I literally **burnt** something that wasn't supposed to burn.

Old me would have spent **weeks** obsessing over how embarrassing it was.

New me? I laughed about it, reminded myself **even top chefs have disasters**, and moved on.

Because at the end of the day, **being kind to yourself is the only way to survive life's bloopers.**

Step 3: Never Berate Yourself (Seriously, Cut That Out)

If I had a rupee for every time I **insulted myself inside my head**, I'd have enough to retire on a private island.

I've called myself:

- *"So stupid."*

- *"Such a mess."*

- *"A failure at life."*

And for what? **Making normal human mistakes?**

Look, **nobody is perfect.** But constantly putting yourself down is like trying to swim with a backpack full of bricks. **You won't get anywhere.**

So here's what I started doing instead:

- **Whenever I made a mistake, I replaced the self-criticism with self-compassion.**

   Instead of *"Wow, I'm terrible at this"*, I said *"I'll get better with practice."*

- **Whenever I felt unworthy, I reminded myself of my strengths.**

   "Okay, today was rough, but you're still an incredible human."

And let me tell you—**this shift changed my entire outlook on life.**

Step 4: Own Your Anxieties Instead of Running from Them

Let's be real—**anxiety is like that annoying neighbor who keeps showing up uninvited.**

You can pretend it doesn't exist. You can try to block it out. But eventually, it **finds a way in.**

For years, I **ran from my anxieties.**

o   I ignored them.

o   I distracted myself.

o   I convinced myself **if I pretended to be fine, I would magically be fine.**

Guess what? **It didn't work.**

The only thing that did work? **Facing my anxiety head-on.**

Instead of avoiding my fears, I started **acknowledging them.**

o   *"Okay, I feel anxious right now. That's okay."*

o   *"Yes, this situation is scary, but I can handle it."*

o   *"I've survived 100% of my bad days so far—I can survive this too."*

Owning your anxiety **takes away its power.** It stops being this **huge, uncontrollable monster** and becomes just **another part of you that you're learning to manage.**

Step 5: Protect Your Energy Like Your Life Depends on It (Reflect on this!)

Do you ever feel **drained** after spending time with certain people?

Like, you meet them **full of energy**, and by the time they leave, you feel like **a deflated balloon**?

That's because **not everyone deserves access to your energy.**

I used to say yes to **everyone.**

o   Yes to people who drained me.

o   Yes to situations that stressed me out.

o   Yes to relationships that didn't serve me.

And it left me **exhausted**.

So I learned to set **boundaries.**

o   I stopped **hanging out with people wh**o only brought negativity.

o   I stopped over-explaining myself to those who wouldn't understand.

o   I stopped **feeling guilty for choosing my peace.**

And wow—**life got so much better.**

Final Thoughts: You Are the Reflection of What You Receive

At the end of the day, **the way you treat yourself sets the standard for how others will treat you.**

o   **Want respect? Start respecting yourself first.**

o   **Want love? Start loving yourself first.**

o   **Want peace? Start creating it within yourself first.**

Because if **you don't show up for yourself, no one else will.**

So, let this be the moment you decide to:

✓ Be your own biggest supporter.

✓ Talk to yourself with kindness.

✓ Own your anxieties instead of running from them.

✓ Set boundaries that protect your peace.

Because at the end of the day, **you are your own safe space.**

And when you truly believe that, **you'll never feel lost again.**

The Magic of Routine for an Anxious Mind

I don't know about you, but if left to my own devices, my mind has the ability to create absolute chaos within minutes. One second, I'm thinking about what to cook for lunch, and the next, I'm spiraling into a full-blown existential crisis about whether I saved enough for retirement or if I should've picked a different career altogether. It's like my brain enjoys playing KBC but with only anxiety-inducing questions and no lifelines.

And that's exactly why I have a structured routine in place. Not because I have my life together (let's not kid ourselves), but because without it, I'm one missed WhatsApp notification away from panic mode.

So, let me introduce you to something that has truly saved me from drowning in my own thoughts:

MAKERS –

Meditation,

Affirmations,

Keeping a Journal,

Exercise,

Reading, and

Self-care.

These six pillars of my routine are not just tasks; they are the reason I haven't completely lost my mind.

Now, do you have to follow them in the same order? Not at all. But knowing they exist and that they work is enough to get started. Let's dive in.

M - Meditation: The Art of Sitting Still Without Plotting Your Own Funeral

I used to think meditation was a scam. Sit still, focus on your breath, and magically all problems vanish? Yeah, right. I couldn't sit still for more than 10 seconds before my brain went, "Did I turn off the gas?" or "What if I accidentally sent my boss a message meant for my husband?"

But over time, I realized meditation isn't about **stopping** thoughts—it's about **observing** them and not letting them hijack your emotions. I started small, with guided meditations (thank you, YouTube gurus), and now I can manage 7-10 minutes. That's a world record in my books.

I also practice **chakra meditation** and **Ho'oponopono meditation**, which sound fancy but are basically ways to tell my overthinking brain, "Calm down, we're safe." It's like giving my mind a warm hug every morning.

Pro tip: If sitting in silence seems impossible, start with walking meditation. Walk in circles, pretend you're deep in thought (Bollywood hero style), and focus on your breath. You'll look mysterious AND reduce anxiety. Win-win!

A - Affirmations: Talking to Yourself But in a Productive Way

Affirmations used to feel ridiculous. I mean, standing in front of a mirror and saying, "I am strong, I am calm, I am enough" felt like I was auditioning for a motivational speaker role.

But then I noticed something strange. The more I repeated these phrases, the less I believed the nonsense my anxiety was trying to sell me. I was no longer feeding the "What if I fail?" thoughts—I was countering them with, "Even if I fail, I'll learn and grow."

So now, affirmations are a non-negotiable part of my routine. If I can spend years believing my anxiety's lies, I can definitely spend a few minutes believing positive truths about myself.

Try this: Write 3-5 affirmations and stick them where you'll see them daily—fridge, bathroom mirror, inside your laptop cover.

My personal favorites:

"All is always well in my life."

"This too shall Pass".

"I can do this!!".

K - Keeping a Journal: The Brain Dump That Saves Lives

Journaling is my therapy, my personal TED talk, and my brain's junk drawer—all in one. I already told you all about it in the previous chapter.

Let me tell you, the first time I started writing, I had NO idea what to write. "Dear diary, today I ate dal chawal" wasn't exactly groundbreaking.

But soon, it became a safe space to **acknowledge, accept, and love myself.** I wasn't trying to fix myself—I was trying to understand myself.

Now, journaling helps me:

- ✓ **Process my emotions** before they explode

- ✓ **Catch negative thought patterns** before they spiral

- ✓ **Rant freely** without scaring my husband

Hack: If writing feels hard, start with bullet points. Just list how you feel. Some days my journal entry is literally: **"Today sucked. I want to scream. But I won't. Okay, maybe just a little."** And that's okay.

E - Exercise: Moving So You Don't Murder Someone

If anxiety could be shaken off like water, exercise would be the towel.

I don't exercise to lose weight. I exercise to **not lose my mind**. When I do yoga, I feel like a Zen monk (even if my downward dog looks like a struggling cat). When I walk, I get my best ideas (or overanalyze past conversations, but let's pretend it's productive). And when I dance? Oh, that's when I truly stop caring.

Movement brings fresh oxygen to the brain, which means fewer panic attacks and more clarity. Plus, after a workout, I feel so accomplished that even if I do nothing else that day, I can say, **"At least I exercised."**

Hack: If you hate traditional workouts, try **Bollywood dance therapy**—put on your favorite song and **dance like no one's watching**. Unless they are watching, in which case, give them a full performance!

R - Reading: Feeding the Brain Something Other Than Anxiety

Anxious minds need **inputs** that aren't just overthinking. Reading gives me a break from my own thoughts and lets me borrow someone else's (preferably a well-adjusted person's).

I read books on **mindfulness, self-improvement, and fiction**—because sometimes, escaping into a fantasy world is the best therapy.

And no, it doesn't have to be a deep, intellectual book. Even a **masala-filled thriller** works, as long as it keeps your brain busy with something other than *"What did that text really mean?"*

Pro tip: If reading is too much, listen to audiobooks while cooking, walking, or pretending to work. Multitasking at its finest!

S - Self-Care: More Than Just Face Masks and Spa Days

Self-care isn't always glamorous. Sometimes, it's **cleaning my closet** so my surroundings don't add to my stress. Sometimes, it's **deleting 2000 emails** so I don't have a mini heart attack every time I open my inbox.

It's also setting **boundaries**—saying NO to things that drain me, even if it makes people uncomfortable. Because let's be honest, if I say yes to everyone, I'll end up crying in a corner from exhaustion.

And most importantly, self-care is about **being kind to myself**. No self-shaming, no guilt trips, just **acceptance and care**.

Bonus: EFT Tapping & Visualization

Some days, my routine alone isn't enough. That's when I turn to **EFT tapping** (gently tapping on energy points while repeating affirmations) and **visualization** (picturing myself in a calm, happy place).

Both work wonders when anxiety is hitting hard and I need a quick fix.

Final Thoughts: MAKERS = Sanity Saver

This routine **doesn't erase anxiety**, but it makes it **manageable**. On tough days, it's my anchor. On good days, it's my reminder to stay grounded.

So, to anyone reading this: **Find your MAKERS. Adapt it. Make it your own. And most importantly, stick to it—because your mind deserves peace, and YOU deserve a life that isn't ruled by anxiety.**

Now, go forth and make your anxious mind a little less chaotic. And if all else fails, **dance like no one's watching.**

Financial and Emotional Independence: The Power of Standing on Your Own Two Feet (Without Wobbling Too Much)

Let's get one thing straight—being independent doesn't mean you suddenly become a superhero who never needs help. It just means that **whether or not someone else shows up, you'll be just fine**. And let me tell you, there's a kind of peace that comes with that realization—like finally clearing your WhatsApp unread messages or finding money in an old purse.

Now, we're talking about two types of independence here: **financial** (because relying on someone else's wallet is a dangerous game) and **emotional** (because relying on someone else's approval is even worse). The goal is to reach a point where your happiness and stability aren't tied to another person, a paycheck, or whether your best friend texts back within five minutes.

Sounds good? Let's break it down.

Step 1: Money = Freedom (Even If You Hate Math)

You don't have to be a finance wizard or enjoy reading investment books that put you to sleep. But you do need to know the basics of money, because **financial independence is not about being rich—it's about having choices.**

Financial Independence for Homemakers (Yes, Even If You Don't Earn Yet!)

If you're a homemaker who isn't currently making money, it's easy to feel financially dependent. But guess what? **There are still ways to build financial security, even before you start earning.**

1. Manage the Household Budget Like a CFO

Your home is your company, and you are the Chief Financial Officer. Track income, expenses, savings, and investments like a pro. When you **know where the money is going, you have power.**

2. Have a Separate Bank Account

Even if you don't earn, having a **personal bank account** helps you get into the habit of managing money. Start by putting aside a small amount every month.

3. Build an Emergency Fund

Start with whatever you can—□500, □1,000 a month. Over time, it adds up and gives you **security and confidence.**

4. Learn About Investments

Even if someone else handles the finances, **know where the money is invested.** Understanding mutual funds, fixed deposits, or even gold investments can make a huge difference.

5. Find a Way to Start Earning (Even Small Amounts!)

Financial independence starts when you have **your own income.** If you're looking for ways to earn from home, here are some ideas:

- o **Freelancing:** Writing, graphic design, video editing, or social media management.

- o **Teaching or Coaching:** Online tuition, yoga, baking, or even life coaching.

o **Selling Handmade Products**: Jewelry, soaps, candles, or home décor.

o **Home-Based Food Business**: Catering, baking, or selling specialty snacks.

o **Affiliate Marketing**: Recommend products online and earn commissions.

o **Reselling Products**: Buy in bulk and sell online or within your community.

o **Blogging or YouTube**: If you love sharing knowledge, create content and monetize it.

o **Online Surveys & Market Research**: It won't make you rich, but it's a small income stream.

Even if you start small, **earning even ₹5,000-₹10,000 per month can give you confidence and independence.**

The "I Don't Want to Think About It" Guide to Financial Independence

If money talk makes you anxious, here's a simple approach:

o **Know What's Coming In and Going Out**

    o You don't need a fancy budgeting app. A simple list of how much is coming in and where it's going is enough. Ignoring your finances doesn't make them better.

o **Save Like Your Future Self Will Thank You**

    o Even if it's just a few hundred rupees a month, **start saving now.** Future-you will appreciate it when you have a cushion to fall back on.

- o **Invest, Don't Just Save**

  - o Saving is good. But **investing is better** because inflation eats up savings like your favorite snack. Start with simple things—mutual funds, fixed deposits, or even gold.

- o **Learn a New Skill That Can Earn Money**

  - o If you have free time, upskill yourself! Learn digital marketing, social media management, or baking—anything that can bring in money.

Bottom Line: **You don't need millions to be financially independent. You just need to be in control of what you have.**

Step 2: Emotional Independence – Your Happiness Shouldn't Be in Someone Else's Hands

Okay, now that we've covered money, let's talk about something even trickier: **your emotions.**

Most of us have been conditioned to believe that our happiness is tied to someone else—our partner, our family, our friends. But here's the truth: **the moment your happiness depends on someone else's actions, you've lost control of your own life.**

How to Build Emotional Independence

- o **Be Your Own Cheerleader**

  - o Stop waiting for someone else to say, "You did a great job!" Look in the mirror and tell yourself that **YOU ARE AWESOME.** (Yes, you'll feel ridiculous at first. Do it anyway.)

- o **Learn to Sit with Your Own Company**

  - o If the thought of having a solo coffee date makes you nervous, start small. Take a walk alone, eat at a restaurant by yourself, or watch a movie solo. The goal? **To become comfortable with your own presence.**

o **Detach from Other People's Opinions**

  o People will always have something to say. But **their opinions don't pay your bills or define your worth.**

o **Set Boundaries and Stick to Them**

  o If someone drains your energy, limit your time with them. If a situation makes you uncomfortable, say no. Boundaries aren't rude; **they're necessary for your peace.**

o **Don't Rely on a Relationship for Happiness**

  o A partner should **add** to your happiness, not be the source of it. If your self-worth crumbles the moment someone leaves, it's a sign that you need to build a stronger foundation within yourself.

Hacks to Stay Emotionally Strong

✓ **Journaling**—Write down your feelings so they don't bottle up.

✓ **Meditation & Affirmations**—Because your brain needs positive reinforcement, not just overthinking.

✓ **Find Your Tribe**—A few real friends who support you are worth more than a crowd of people who don't.

Bottom Line: **You are responsible for your own happiness. Take that power back.**

The Magic Combo: Financial + Emotional Independence

Now, imagine combining the two. Imagine waking up one day knowing that:

- ✓ **You don't need anyone else's money to live comfortably.**

- ✓ **You don't need anyone else's approval to feel good about yourself.**

That's true **FREEDOM**.

And guess what? **It's possible.** It just takes small, consistent actions.

Quickfire Tips to Get There Faster

- **Start saving today. Even if it's ₹500 a month.**

- **Learn basic investing—because your money should work for you.**

- **Practice saying no. Your time and energy are valuable.**

- **Do something alone every week—coffee, a movie, a walk.**

- **Celebrate small wins. Your progress matters.**

Final Thoughts: You Are Your Own Backup Plan

At the end of the day, **being financially and emotionally independent isn't about cutting yourself off from others—it's about knowing that you'll be okay no matter what.**

It's about walking into life with the confidence of someone who knows they can take care of themselves, whether it's paying their own bills or managing their own emotions.

And trust me, **that kind of confidence is priceless.**

So go on, take charge. Your future self is already cheering you on.

Finding Purpose: Turning Pain into Passion

If someone had told me years ago that **my greatest struggles would lead me to my purpose**, I would have probably rolled my eyes and gone back to stress-eating a plate of pani puri. At the time, my pain felt like a permanent resident in my life, not a stepping stone to something meaningful.

But life has a funny way of proving us wrong, doesn't it?

Now, I look back and realize that **every tear, every sleepless night, every anxiety attack, every "I can't do this" moment actually prepared me for the work I do today**—helping people heal through food, lifestyle changes, and emotional well-being. What once felt like random suffering now makes perfect sense. **It was all leading me somewhere.**

If you're feeling lost, stuck, or like life has just thrown you into the deep end **without a life jacket**, hang in there. Because your pain isn't pointless—it might just be pointing you toward your purpose.

Let's talk about how.

Step 1: Understanding That Pain Isn't a Dead End

When you're in pain—whether it's from anxiety, heartbreak, failure, or something else entirely—it feels **impossible** to think about the future. You're too busy **just trying to survive**.

But here's what I've learned: **Pain isn't the end of the road. It's just a really annoying, unexpected detour.**

Think about it. Some of the most inspiring people in the world—activists, artists, entrepreneurs, healers—didn't wake up one day with a clear mission. **They went through something painful, and instead of letting it destroy them, they transformed it into something powerful.**

For example:

- o A woman who struggled with body image issues becomes a self-love coach.

- o Someone who lost everything in a financial crisis starts teaching others about money management.

- o A person who battled mental health issues creates a community to support others going through the same thing.

Pain doesn't have to be **just pain**. It can be **fuel**.

And if you're thinking, "That sounds great, but I don't know how to do that," don't worry. That's what we're figuring out next.

Step 2: Recognizing the Patterns in Your Pain

What keeps showing up in your life?

- o Do you always find yourself helping others with a specific problem?

- o Is there something you've struggled with that you now know how to navigate?

- o Have you gone through something that completely changed how you see the world?

Your purpose is often **hidden in the patterns of your life.**

For me, my struggles with anxiety, emotional eating, and the chaos of balancing a million things at once **led me to helping others heal through food, self-care, and lifestyle changes.**

At first, I didn't even realize it. I was just trying to figure out how to manage my own life. But as I started sharing what worked for me, people started coming to me for advice. And that's when it hit me—**maybe my struggles weren't just for me. Maybe they were meant to help others too.**

So, ask yourself:

o   What challenges have you overcome?

o   What do people naturally come to you for advice on?

o   What topic or cause makes you feel **something deep inside**?

Your answers might give you a clue about where your purpose lies.

Step 3: Taking the First Small Step (Even If It Feels Silly)

Okay, so you've got an idea of what matters to you. Now what?

Start small.

I didn't wake up one day and say, "I'm going to help people change their lives through food and mindset." I just started experimenting with healthy recipes, journaling about my experiences, and talking to people about what helped me.

You don't need a five-year plan. You just need a **first step**:

o   If you love writing, start a blog or Instagram page.

o   If you want to help people with something, offer advice or create a small workshop.

o   If you're passionate about a cause, volunteer or start a small initiative.

The goal isn't to have it all figured out. **The goal is to just begin.**

And yes, it might feel weird at first. You might doubt yourself. You might hear that little voice in your head saying, "Who do you think you are?"

Ignore it. **Do it anyway.**

Step 4: Turning Passion Into Something Bigger

Once you start, you'll notice something incredible—**when you do what truly aligns with you, things start falling into place.**

o   Opportunities appear.

o   People connect with what you're doing.

o   You feel more energized, even on tough days.

But here's the thing—your passion isn't just about making money or building a career (although, that can be a nice bonus!). **It's about impact.**

The best part? **You don't have to quit everything and go "find yourself" in the mountains.** You can integrate your purpose into your existing life.

For example:

o   If you're passionate about mental health, start a podcast or a support group.

o   If you love fitness, begin by training a few friends before launching a full business.

o   If you're into sustainability, educate people through social media or local workshops.

Passion doesn't have to be a **huge, life-changing project** from day one. **It grows over time.**

Step 5: Learning to Trust Yourself (Even When It's Hard)

This might be the toughest step of all. Because the second you start pursuing something meaningful, **self-doubt will come knocking.**

o   "What if I fail?"

o   "What if no one cares?"

o   "What if I'm not good enough?"

Let me tell you something—**every single person who has ever done anything great has had these thoughts.**

The difference? They kept going anyway.

Your purpose isn't about perfection. **It's about trying, failing, learning, and trying again.**

Final Thoughts: Your Pain Has Power

If there's one thing I want you to take away from this, it's this: **The things that broke you can also build you.**

Your pain doesn't define you. Your struggles don't make you weak. **They make you uniquely qualified to help others who are going through the same thing.**

And if you're still in the messy middle—where nothing makes sense yet—**that's okay.** Keep going. Keep learning. Keep experimenting.

Because one day, you'll look back and realize that **every single struggle was leading you to something bigger.**

So, take the first step. **Your purpose is waiting.**

Chapter 8

Dealing with Setbacks

When Life Feels Like One Long Panic Attack

(And How to Survive Without Turning into a Puddle of Anxiety)

Some people say life is a rollercoaster. I say life is more like sitting on a rollercoaster that you *thought* was a kiddie ride—safe, predictable, and maybe even fun—only for it to suddenly drop you into a 360-degree loop while someone throws tax bills, deadlines, and unexpected phone calls your way. Oh, and did I mention the seatbelt feels a little loose?

That's how my brain processes setbacks. While some people can take challenges in stride, assess the situation logically, and move forward like well-adjusted human beings, my brain prefers to react as if I've been thrown into an apocalyptic survival game. I don't just get upset; I **catastrophize** (as we covered in an earlier chapter) A minor mistake feels like a career-ending failure. A small argument with a loved one convinces me they secretly hate me. A slow week in my cloud kitchen? Clearly, I'm doomed for bankruptcy.

It's not rational, but that's anxiety for you.

The Moment When Panic Takes Over

Some days, I feel like I'm *winning* at life. I wake up early, get my meditation in, tick off my to-do list, and feel like one of those successful people who have their lives together. And then, out of nowhere, **BAM—something happens.**

Let's take a real example. A while back, I hosted an online SHARAN India workshop. I had prepared extensively, planned every single detail, and was sure it would be a great session. But then, **one participant sent a slightly negative message** about how the session wasn't what they expected.

Most people would read it, maybe feel a little bad, and move on. But my anxiety-ridden brain? Oh no. That one comment **became my entire reality.**

- *What if more people felt this way but didn't say it?*

- *What if I'm losing my touch?*

- *What if this is the beginning of my professional downfall?!*

I re-read that message **at least 15 times**, trying to decode hidden meanings that weren't even there. Then, for the next two hours, I spiraled into self-doubt. My heart raced, my stomach twisted into knots, and my mind convinced me that I had officially failed at life.

Was this logical? Absolutely not. Did my brain care? Also no.

How Anxiety Tricks You Into Believing the Worst

The funny part is, I *know* I always get through these moments. I *know* setbacks are a part of life, and I *know* that no single event defines my entire existence. But in the heat of an anxious spiral, my brain refuses to accept this logic.

Instead, it goes straight into **worst-case-scenario mode**. It's like having an overenthusiastic drama director in my head yelling, *"More intensity! More despair! Act like the world is ending!"*

For example, when my cloud kitchen once received a less-than-stellar review, my brain immediately decided:

o   **Nobody will ever order from me again.**

o   **I should shut it all down immediately.**

o   **I have officially ruined my career.**

Now, logically, I know that one review doesn't define my business. But in that moment, my emotions were so overwhelming that logic *didn't matter.* The stress, the fear, and the sheer weight of self-doubt felt real, even if the thoughts weren't true.

What Panic Physically Feels Like

Anxiety isn't just mental—it's physical. When I start panicking, my body **fully commits** to the meltdown:

o   My chest tightens like someone has wrapped a belt around it.

o   My hands get clammy, and I can't seem to warm them up.

o   My breathing turns into rapid, shallow gasps, making me feel even worse.

o   My stomach twists itself into an Olympic-level gymnastics routine.

o   My brain? It decides to replay *every single failure from my past* just for fun.

It's exhausting. And if I don't actively *do something* to stop it, I can get stuck in this cycle for **hours.**

The Science of a Panic Attack (a.k.a. When Your Brain Betrays You)

A panic attack is like an overenthusiastic alarm system that goes off when it **doesn't need to.** Imagine your smoke detector starts screaming just because you lit a scented candle. That's your brain on anxiety.

Here's what happens:

o   Your **amygdala** (the fear center of your brain) detects a "threat." It doesn't matter if it's a real threat like an actual fire or something like a rude email—it reacts the same way.

o   Your body floods with **adrenaline and cortisol.** This is why you feel shaky, breathless, and like you're about to pass out.

o   Your heart rate spikes, your chest tightens, and your stomach twists into knots.

o   Your brain starts sending **doomsday thoughts.** *"This is it. Everything is over. I will never recover from this."*

o   You either go into **fight, flight, or freeze mode.** (I personally specialize in freeze, followed by stress eating if it's work-related and starving if it's financial stress.)

The good news? **You can hijack this response.** Let's talk about how.

How to Bounce Back Without Breaking Down- How I've Learned to Stop the Spiral

Over the years, I've realised that **waiting for the anxiety to go away on its own is NOT a strategy.** I have to take **action** to pull myself out of it. Here's what I do:

How to Talk Yourself Out of an Anxiety Spiral

Your brain is like an overdramatic friend who **needs to be reasoned with.** Here's what I tell myself when I feel a panic attack coming on:

1. Talk to Myself Like I'd Talk to a Friend

When my brain starts its dramatic meltdown, I ask myself, *"Would I say this to a friend?"*

If my best friend told me she was feeling like a failure because of one bad review or a single setback, I wouldn't say, *"Yep, you're doomed forever."* I'd remind her that **one moment doesn't define her.**

So why is it okay to be so harsh with myself?

Now, when anxiety tries to convince me I'm failing at life, I respond like a rational, kind friend:

o *"Okay, this moment sucks. But it's just a moment."*

o *"You've been through worse and survived."*

o *"One bad review, one mistake, one bad day doesn't erase all your successes."*

It doesn't make the anxiety disappear instantly, but it **stops the spiral from getting worse.**

2. Breathe Like a Human (Not a Drowning Goldfish)

When I panic, my breathing turns into shallow, rapid gasps—**which only makes the anxiety worse.**

So, I force myself to do **4-7-8 breathing:**

o Inhale for **4 seconds**

o Hold for **7 seconds**

o Exhale for **8 seconds**

This forces my body to **slow down**, which signals my brain that I'm not actually in danger.

3. Move My Body to Reset My Mind

Anxiety gets trapped in the body, and the fastest way to release it is **movement.**

- o   If I'm home, I'll do a few yoga stretches.

- o   If I'm outside, I'll take a brisk walk.

- o   If I have the energy, I put on music and dance like no one's watching.

It sounds ridiculous, but **movement forces my nervous system to reset.**

4. Ground Myself in Reality

When I'm deep in an anxiety spiral, I feel disconnected from the real world. So, I use the **5-4-3-2-1 grounding technique:**

- o   **5 things I can see**

- o   **4 things I can touch**

- o   **3 things I can hear**

- o   **2 things I can smell**

- o   **1 thing I can taste**

This pulls me *out* of my head and *into* the present moment.

5. Remind Myself: "I Have Survived Every Panic Attack Before"

Every single time I thought, *"This is it, I'll never recover from this,"* guess what?

I did.

I have survived **100%** of my worst days.

And that means I'll survive this one too.

Reframing Failures as Growth

(How to Stop Taking Setbacks Personally and Start Using Them as a Superpower)

Let's be real—**failure sucks**. Nobody enjoys falling flat on their face, whether it's in business, relationships, or personal growth. It stings. It makes you question yourself. It brings up that ugly little voice in your head whispering, *"See? I told you you weren't good enough."*

But here's what I've learned over the years: **failure is not a judgment—it's information.** It's the universe's way of redirecting you, showing you what doesn't work so you can get closer to what *does.*

This perspective shift didn't come naturally to me. Oh no, I had to **fight my brain** every step of the way. My natural tendency has always been to overanalyse, overreact, and let failures shake my confidence. But over time, through trial, error, and a lot of **panicked journaling sessions**, I realised that failure is a crucial part of the process.

Let me share some of my personal failures—some hilarious, some painful—and how they ended up teaching me far more than my successes ever did.

That Time My Cloud Kitchen Launch Flopped (And How I Saved It)

A few years ago, I was **SO excited** about launching a new menu for my cloud kitchen. I had spent *weeks* perfecting the dishes, designing the marketing, and building up expectations in my head. I imagined people **raving** about it, orders flying in, and me basking in the glory of my culinary genius.

But then… **nothing happened.**

The orders were **shockingly low**. The feedback? **Less than glowing.** And my confidence? **Crushed.**

My first reaction? **Panic.**

My second reaction? **Self-doubt.**

I started questioning **everything**:

o   *Was this a bad idea?*

o   *Do I even know what I'm doing?*

o   *Maybe I should just shut everything down and become a hermit in the mountains.*

But after I calmed down (and ate my body weight in comfort food), I forced myself to look at the situation **logically**.

Instead of treating it as proof that I was a failure, I asked myself:

o   *What exactly went wrong?*

o   *Was it the menu? The pricing? The marketing?*

o   *Did I really give it enough time before declaring it a failure?*

After analyzing, I realized:

o   **I hadn't marketed it well enough.** People didn't even know about the new menu!

o   **The pricing was slightly off.** Some items were perceived as too expensive.

o   **The dishes I thought would be hits… weren't.** But others, which I'd barely promoted, were actually doing well.

So, instead of sulking, I **made adjustments**—tweaked the marketing, refined the pricing, and focused on the dishes people actually loved. **A month later, sales picked up.** Two months later, the new menu became a success.

The initial failure **wasn't a reflection of me—it was a reflection of what didn't work.** That's it.

Failure Isn't the End — It's a Detour

When something doesn't work out, it's so easy to take it *personally*. We assume it means:

o   *We're not good enough.*

o   *We're not capable.*

o   *We should probably just give up.*

But in reality, failure isn't a sign that you're doomed. **It's a redirection.** It's the universe saying, *"Hey, that wasn't the right path, but let me guide you to a better one."*

I can't tell you how many times I've looked back at something I thought was a *massive* failure and realized it was actually **saving me from something worse** or leading me to something better.

For example:

o   **A job rejection that crushed me at the time… but freed me up for a much better opportunity a few months later.**

o   **A friendship that fell apart… but made space for deeper, healthier relationships in my life.**

o   **A failed project that felt humiliating… but ended up teaching me skills I needed for an even bigger success later.**

Every single time, I came out *stronger*—even if I couldn't see it at the moment.

The Three-Step Mindset Shift to Reframe Failure

Over time, I've developed a **simple process** to help me deal with failure without spiralling into self-doubt and existential crises. It's not magic, but it **works.**

Step 1: Detach Emotion and Look at the Data

When something goes wrong, **take your emotions out of it** (as much as possible) and look at the raw facts.

Instead of saying, *"I failed because I'm not good enough,"* ask:

o   *What exactly didn't work?*

o   *Were there factors outside my control?*

o   *What could I have done differently?*

For example, instead of thinking, *"Nobody likes my cooking,"* I realised my cloud kitchen launch flopped because I hadn't **marketed properly.**

That's **data**, not failure.

Step 2: Extract the Lesson (Without Self-Judgment)

Once you've figured out what went wrong, ask yourself:

o   *What is this experience trying to teach me?*

o   *How can I use this knowledge to improve?*

Sometimes, the lesson is **strategic** (like adjusting my pricing). Other times, it's **emotional** (like learning to trust myself more). Either way, failure is a **teacher**, not a punishment.

Step 3: Apply What You've Learned and Try Again

Now comes the hardest part: **getting back up.**

It's tempting to **avoid trying again** after a failure. But the only way to grow is to **use what you've learned and make another attempt.**

o   If you failed at a business idea, **tweak it and try again.**

o   If you bombed a presentation, **improve your preparation and do another one.**

o   If you had a bad experience in a relationship, **reflect on what went wrong and approach the next one with more wisdom.**

The "Failing Forward" Mindset

The most successful people in the world **fail all the time—**they just **don't let failure stop them.**

Think about it: (All 3 are my favourite people- total inspiration)

o   **Oprah Winfrey** was fired from her first TV job and told she wasn't meant for television.

o   **Walt Disney** was told he "lacked imagination" and was fired from a newspaper job.

o   **J.K. Rowling** was rejected **12 times** before *Harry Potter* got published.

Imagine if any of them had let failure define them.

Failure is only **permanent** if you stop trying. But if you use it as a learning tool, it actually **pushes you forward.**

Final Thoughts: Failure Isn't the Opposite of Success — It's Part of It

If there's one thing I hope you take away from this, it's this:

Failure isn't proof that you're not good enough. It's proof that you're learning, growing, and evolving.

The next time you face a setback, **don't let it crush you.** Instead:

- ✓ **Detach from the emotions and look at the facts.**

- ✓ **Extract the lesson and adjust your approach.**

- ✓ **Apply what you've learned and try again.**

And most importantly—**don't take failure personally.** It's not a verdict on your worth. It's just feedback, helping you get closer to success.

So go ahead. Mess up. Learn. Grow. And keep moving forward.

Because the only true failure? **Is giving up.**

Asking for Help: It's Not a Weakness, It's a Power Move

There was a time when I thought asking for help was a **public declaration of failure.** In my head, strong people **figured things out on their own.** They didn't need therapy, didn't cry on the phone to a friend, and certainly didn't admit when they were struggling.

Spoiler alert: I was dead wrong.

I was running on empty, holding everything in, and pretending I was fine. But guess what? That only led to **anxiety spirals, burnout, and emotional breakdowns at the most inconvenient moments (usually in the middle of the grocery store aisle).**

Then, one day, I did the unthinkable. **I asked for help.**

And instead of feeling weak, I felt something I hadn't in a long time— **relief.**

The truth is, **asking for help is not a weakness. It's a power move.** It means you're self-aware enough to know when you need support, and smart enough to go get it. It's what helps you grow, heal, and ultimately thrive.

If you're struggling right now, **please seek help.** Whether it's through therapy, journaling, talking to a trusted friend, or leaning on a support group—you don't have to do this alone.

Let's talk about why seeking help is so important, the different ways you can do it, and how professional help (aka therapy) can be a **game-changer.**

The Lie We Tell Ourselves: "I Should Be Able to Handle This Alone"

There's a **huge stigma** around asking for help, especially when it comes to mental health. Society teaches us to be independent, to "tough it out," and to believe that struggling in silence is some kind of badge of honor.

But let's put this in perspective.

Imagine breaking your leg. Would you:

a. Drag yourself around and pretend you're fine?

b. Call a doctor because, obviously, a broken leg needs medical attention?

If you answered *b* (which I sincerely hope you did), then why wouldn't you treat your **mental health** the same way?

o Feeling overwhelmed? That's like carrying a **backpack full of bricks**—you can put it down.

o Struggling with anxiety? That's like a **car alarm going off**—it's trying to tell you something.

o Drowning in stress? That's like a **leaky pipe**—if you don't fix it, it only gets worse.

Seeking help doesn't mean you're failing. It means you're **taking responsibility for your well-being.**

How Therapy Changed My Life

I won't lie—my first therapy session felt **weird.**

I sat there, unsure of what to say, feeling like an imposter in my own struggles. I even had thoughts like:

o   *What if my problems aren't "big enough" for therapy?*

o   *What if my therapist secretly thinks I'm dramatic?*

o   *What if talking about this makes everything worse?*

But after a few sessions, something clicked. Therapy wasn't about someone **fixing** me (because I was never broken). It was about **understanding myself better**—why I reacted the way I did, why certain situations triggered me, and how I could build healthier thought patterns.

Therapy gave me tools that **completely changed the way I handle stress, anxiety, and setbacks.**

Here are just a few things I learned:

o   **My thoughts aren't always facts.** Just because my brain tells me I'm failing doesn't make it true.

o   **I don't have to react to every emotion.** Sometimes, I just need to sit with them, acknowledge them, and let them pass.

o   **Boundaries are a form of self-care.** Saying "no" to toxic situations is not rude—it's necessary.

Therapy isn't about sitting on a couch and talking about your childhood (unless you want to). It's about **equipping yourself with strategies to handle life better.**

And if therapy feels **intimidating**, there are plenty of other ways to seek help.

Different Ways to Ask for Help (That Don't Involve a Couch and a Therapist)

If you're not ready for therapy, that's okay. Here are some other ways to seek support:

1. Journaling (Your Thoughts Need an Exit Door)

Writing things down helps **declutter your brain** and process emotions without judgment. Some prompts that helped me:

o   *What's weighing on me right now?*

o   *What advice would I give a friend going through this?*

o   *What's one thing I can do today to feel a little better?*

Even if it's just scribbling *"I HAVE NO IDEA WHAT I'M DOING"* ten times, that's still progress.

2. Talking to Trusted Friends (Because Bottling It Up Doesn't Work)

You don't need a **huge** support system—just a few people who genuinely listen and care. Find those people and **be honest**with them.

It's okay to say:

o   *"I'm struggling right now."*

o   *"I just need someone to listen."*

o   *"Can we talk? I don't want to feel alone in this."*

Trust me, real friends **want** to be there for you. Let them.

3. Support Groups (Because Someone Out There Gets It)

Sometimes, talking to people who have **been through the same thing** is incredibly healing. Whether it's an online forum, a local group, or even a WhatsApp community, **connecting with people who understand your struggles can be life-changing.**

How to Keep Moving Forward (Even When You Want to Give Up)

When setbacks hit, it's easy to feel stuck, hopeless, or like you're falling behind. But remember—**setbacks are detours, not dead ends.**

Here's how to keep going, even on the hardest days:

1. Don't Compare Your Journey to Others (Yes, Even on Social Media)

Social media makes it look like **everyone has their life together** except you. But that's a lie. You're only seeing their highlight reel, not their behind-the-scenes struggles.

Your journey is **yours**—and it doesn't have to look like anyone else's.

2. Celebrate Small Wins (Yes, Even Getting Out of Bed Counts)

Progress isn't always **big, dramatic breakthroughs.** Sometimes, it's just:

- ✓ Getting out of bed when you didn't want to.

- ✓ Sending that email you've been avoiding.

- ✓ Choosing to drink water instead of coffee (okay, maybe after one cup).

Small wins add up. Celebrate them.

3. Find Your Support System (Quality Over Quantity)

You don't need a **huge** circle of friends—you just need the **right ones.** Find the people who uplift you, who make you feel safe, and who remind you of your strength when you forget.

4. Take It One Day at a Time (Because Life Is Not a Sprint—It's a Marathon with Snack Breaks)

Some days will be **amazing.** Others will be **messy.** That's life.

You don't have to have everything figured out. Just **focus on today.** Take it one step at a time, one decision at a time.

And when it all feels overwhelming? **Pause. Breathe. Ask for help.**

Because you don't have to do this alone. **And you're stronger than you think.**

Chapter 9

A Day in the Life of an Anxious (But Surprisingly Capable) Person

Anxiety and I have been in a long-term relationship, but that doesn't mean every day is a dramatic spiral into doom. Some days, I have absolute clarity, moments of peace, and even a sense of control over my life. And then, of course, there are the days when I overthink grocery store interactions.

The truth is, being an anxious person doesn't mean my life is an endless loop of panic. I've had incredible, fulfilling moments that make me proud. But let's be real—it also means that small, everyday situations sometimes feel like major events.

So, here's a **real, balanced look at a day in my life**—with all its quirks, overthinking, and surprisingly awesome moments.

7:00 AM – Waking Up: Existential Crisis or a Fresh Start?

Some mornings, I wake up with a sense of purpose. I feel clear-headed, energized, and ready to take on the day. Other mornings… not so much.

On those days, my first thoughts are:

o *Did I forget something important?*

o *Should I be doing more with my life?*

o *Maybe I should move to the mountains and live a simple, peaceful life surrounded by fruit trees.*

But instead of letting those thoughts take over, I've learned to **pause and redirect.** I take a deep breath, remind myself that my brain is just doing its usual morning "warm-up," and start my MAKERS routine—Meditation, Affirmations, Keeping a journal, Exercise, Reading, and Self-care.

Some days, my meditation is **deep and peaceful**. Other days, I spend five minutes thinking about whether I need more avocados. But hey, it's progress.

9:00 AM – A Surprisingly Calm Trip to the Grocery Store-Natures Basket

There was a time when grocery shopping felt like a small social challenge.

o *Do I need a cart or a basket?*

o *Should I greet the cashier or just give a polite nod?*

o *If I see someone I know, do I stop and chat or pretend I didn't notice them?*

But these days, I've learned to **relax into the experience**. Instead of rushing through the store, I take my time. I focus on the bright colors of the produce, pick out the ripest fruit, and enjoy the simple act of choosing nourishing food.

I even **smile at the cashier**—which, a few years ago, felt like an awkward social performance. Now, it's just a normal, human interaction. Growth!

12:00 PM – An WhatsApp Notification (and a Rational Response!)

Ding. An WhatsApp message.

Old me would stare at the notification (if from someone who matters), imagine worst-case scenarios, and put off opening it for hours.

Current me? I take a deep breath, remind myself that **most messages are not life-threatening**, and just **open it.**

And guess what? It's an invitation to a friends meal together from a dear friend and just wants to know my availability .

No crisis necessary.

3:00 PM – Reflecting on How Far I've Come (Stroke Days Edition)

There was a time when a single phone call from the doctor would send me into **panic mode**.

I remember one particular check-up after my stroke. I was convinced that the doctor was going to give me **horrible news**. My heart was pounding, my palms were sweaty, and I was mentally preparing for the worst.

But then, I walked into the room, and the doctor smiled and said, *"You're doing great. Keep taking care of yourself."*

That was it.

I had built up an entire disaster scenario in my head, only for reality to be completely fine. That day taught me a huge lesson: **Most of the time, my anxiety is lying to me.**

Now, when those old fears creep in, I remind myself:

o *I've faced real challenges and come out stronger.*

o *Not every situation requires panic mode.*

o *Sometimes, things actually turn out okay.*

And you know what? That realization has brought me a lot of peace.

6:00 PM – A Productive Work Session (Without Overthinking!)

One of my biggest wins? **Learning to focus on my work without constantly second-guessing myself.**

Whether it's working on a new recipe for my cloud kitchen, planning content for my nutrition workshops, or brainstorming ideas for *Thrive on Fruit*, I've learned that **taking action is the best antidote to anxiety.**

o Instead of doubting every decision, I remind myself: **I know what I'm doing.**

o Instead of waiting for the "perfect" time to start, I just start.

o Instead of worrying about what people will think, I focus on **doing my best.**

And on the days when the self-doubt creeps in? I go back to my affirmations: *I am capable. I am learning. I am growing.*

It may sound simple, but **it works.**

9:00 PM – Winding Down (Without Overthinking the Entire Day)

A few years ago, bedtime used to be **prime overthinking time.**

I'd lie in bed replaying awkward moments from the past, worrying about the future, and generally **torturing myself with unnecessary thoughts.**

But now? I've built **a solid nighttime routine** that helps me actually relax.

o **Journaling**: I write down my thoughts, clear my mind, and remind myself of the good moments from the day.

o **Ho'oponopono meditation**: A beautiful practice that helps me let go of worries and forgive myself for the small things I used to obsess over.

o **Reading**: Instead of scrolling on my phone, I end my day with a few pages of a good book.

And the best part? **I actually sleep well.** (Most nights, anyway.)

Final Thoughts: Anxiety Is Part of My Life, But It Doesn't Control Me

Yes, I still have anxious moments. Yes, I still overthink sometimes. But I also have moments of **clarity, confidence, and joy**.

I've learned that:

o **Anxiety doesn't define me.**

o **Small daily wins matter.**

o **I am more resilient than I think.**

And if you're someone who struggles with anxiety, let me tell you this: **You're doing better than you think.**

You're not failing. You're growing. You're learning. And every time you face a challenge and keep moving forward, **you're proving to yourself just how strong you really are.**

Chapter 10

Diet Log of an Anxious Person

(A Whole-Food Plant-Based Approach to Nourish the Nervous System)

Anxiety affects more than just our thoughts—it influences our digestion, energy levels, and even our cravings. As someone who understands both anxiety and nutrition, I know how crucial it is to **eat in a way that calms the nervous system rather than overstimulating it.**

A diet rich in **whole, plant-based foods** provides steady energy, stabilizes blood sugar levels, and supports gut health—all of which directly impact our mood and anxiety levels.

Here's a **daily meal plan** designed to help manage anxiety while keeping meals delicious, wholesome, and satisfying.

Daily Meal Structure

- o **Morning Herbal Infusion (Upon Waking Up) Any 1**

  1. Peppermint tea (calming for digestion)

  2. Tulsi (holy basil) tea (reduces stress hormones)

  3. Lemon water with a pinch of pink salt (hydration + mineral balance)

o **Breakfast: Nutrient-Dense Start**

1. Green smoothie with banana, spinach, and coconut water

2. Chopped seasonal fruits with a sprinkle of chia seeds

o **Mid-Morning Hydration & Light Snack**

1. Fresh coconut water (rich in electrolytes and calming minerals)

2. Lemon water with soaked chia seeds

3. A handful of soaked almonds & walnuts

o **Lunch: A Wholesome, Balanced Meal**

1. A large salad with colorful vegetables, sprouts, and a tahini dressing

2. Steamed vegetables with quinoa or millet

3. Dal (lentils) with red rice or amaranth roti

4. A simple dessert: date and walnut energy balls or a chia seed pudding

o **Afternoon Snack (Keeping Energy Levels Stable) Any 1**

1. Fresh fruit (papaya, apple, or pear)

2. A smoothie with berries, banana and mint leaves

3. Oil-free, grain-free snacks like baked sweet potato chips or flax crackers

o **Dinner: Light, Easy to Digest, and Comforting**

1. A warm bowl of vegetable soup with lentils and greens

2. A meal-replacement salad with avocado, chickpeas, and lemon dressing

3. A grain-free dish like cauliflower rice stir-fry with tofu

o **Before Bed: Relaxing Herbal Tea Any 1**

1. Chamomile tea (calms the mind, improves sleep)

2. Lavender tea (reduces nervous system overstimulation)

3. Golden milk (turmeric, nut milk, and a pinch of cinnamon)

7-Day Anxiety-Friendly Meal Plan

Day	Morning Infusion	Breakfast	Mid-Morning	Lunch	Snack	Dinner	Bedtime Drink
Monday	Peppermint tea	Green smoothie (banana, spinach, flaxseeds)	Coconut water	Quinoa salad, lentil dal, steamed veggies	Papaya slices with soaked walnuts	Vegetable soup + chickpea stir-fry	Chamomile tea
Tuesday	Lemon water	Chopped fruits with chia & almonds	Lemon water with chia	Millet roti, chana masala, cucumber salad	Berry smoothie with sunflower seeds	Warm pumpkin soup + avocado salad	Lavender tea
Wednesday	Tulsi tea	Overnight oats with almond milk & dates	Soaked almonds & walnuts	Amaranth roti, mung bean curry, green salad	Baked sweet potato fries	Cauliflower rice stir-fry with tofu	Golden milk
Thursday	Cinnamon tea	Green smoothie (mango, spinach, hemp seeds)	Fresh coconut water	Brown rice, rajma, beetroot salad	Apple slices with peanut butter	Carrot ginger soup + steamed greens	Chamomile tea
Friday	Lemon water	Chia pudding with berries & nuts	Lemon water with mint	Red rice, vegetable sambar, raw veggie salad	Flaxseed crackers with hummus	Roasted pumpkin soup + stir-fried mushrooms	Lavender tea
Saturday	Peppermint tea	Smoothie bowl (banana, berries, hemp seeds)	Soaked dates & almonds	Buckwheat pancakes with almond butter, side salad	Mango slices with coconut flakes	Tomato soup + quinoa-stuffed bell peppers	Golden milk
Sunday	Ginger turmeric tea	Chopped tropical fruits with flaxseeds	Fresh coconut water	Millet pulao, mixed veg curry, sprout salad	Banana with dark cacao nibs	Miso soup + stir-fried greens with tofu	Chamomile tea

Key Benefits of This Meal Plan for Anxiety

- o **Balanced Blood Sugar Levels**: No sudden crashes that trigger stress hormones.

- o **Rich in Magnesium**: Found in nuts, seeds, greens—helps relax the nervous system.

- o **Gut-Health Friendly**: Probiotic-rich foods like sprouts, fermented veggies, and fiber support the gut-brain axis.

- o **Anti-Inflammatory**: Ingredients like turmeric, flaxseeds, and ginger help reduce inflammation, which is linked to anxiety.

- o **Hydrating & Nourishing**: Herbal teas and coconut water help restore minerals and calm the nervous system.

This meal plan is **not just about eating for anxiety—it's about eating for overall well-being**. Every meal is designed to **nourish the mind, body, and gut** while keeping things delicious and fulfilling.

Chapter 11

Thriving, Not Just Surviving

From Victim to Victor: Shifting the Mindset

There was a time when anxiety dictated everything I did. It wasn't just a feeling; it was a constant presence, a shadow that followed me everywhere. Decisions were made based on fear—fear of failing, fear of judgment, fear of disappointing others. I used to believe that if I was anxious about something, it meant I couldn't handle it. That anxiety was a sign of weakness. That I was doomed to stay stuck in a cycle of stress, overthinking, and self-doubt forever.

But I was wrong.

The biggest shift happened when I stopped seeing myself as a victim of my anxiety and started seeing myself as someone who could work with it. I am still an anxious person—I overthink, I spiral, I still get those heart-racing moments where I'm convinced the world is ending. But the difference is, now, I don't let those moments define me.

Instead of asking, *"Why is this happening to me?"* I started asking, *"What can I learn from this?"*

Instead of assuming, *"I'll never get better,"* I started telling myself, *"I'm working on it, and that's enough."*

And that shift—from helpless to hopeful—is everything.

The Balance Between Healing and Just Living

Let's be honest: healing is exhausting. There are days when I am all in—doing my MAKERS routine, journaling, meditating, practicing EFT tapping, eating mindfully, and setting boundaries like a boss. And then there are days when I just want to curl up in bed with a bowl of baked chips/millet puffs, ignore every self-care practice I've ever learned, and binge-watch something ridiculous.

And you know what? Both are okay.

Healing is not about perfection. It's not a straight road where you suddenly reach a magical destination called "Completely Healed and Forever Happy." It's messy. Some days, you'll feel like you've figured it all out, and other days, you'll feel like you're back to square one. The key is to not beat yourself up over it.

For a long time, I thought healing meant erasing my anxiety. Now I realize, it's not about getting rid of it—it's about learning to live with it in a way that allows me to still be *me*.

There is space for both: working on myself and just existing as I am.

Celebrating Progress, No Matter How Small

There was a time when even saying "no" to something I didn't want to do felt impossible. Now, I do it *most* of the time. (Not always, because let's be real, the people-pleaser in me is still alive and well.)

There was a time when a small setback—like a bad review on my cloud kitchen or an unsuccessful SHARAN workshop—would send me into a spiral of self-doubt for weeks. Now, it stings, but I pick myself up faster.

There was a time when I thought asking for help was a sign of weakness. Now, I know it's one of the strongest things you can do. Therapy is really helping me to find my stable ground and speak about issues I never wanted to address.

These things might seem small to someone else, but to me, they are everything. And that's why I celebrate them. Because every time I choose to take care of myself, to be kinder to myself, to not let anxiety win—that is a victory.

If you're waiting for a *big* moment to feel proud of yourself, stop. Progress is made in the tiny moments. Celebrate them.

Got out of bed on a tough day? That's a win.

Drank water when you felt like skipping meals? That's a win.

Said no to something that drained your energy? That's a win.

Didn't panic when things went off-plan? *Major* win.

I don't wait for the world to validate my progress anymore. I give myself that validation, and it's enough.

Final Thoughts: Embracing Your Beautiful, Anxious Self

If there's one thing I've learned in this journey, it's that I don't need to be "fixed." I am not broken. And neither are you.

Anxiety is part of me, but it does not define me. I am still independent. I am still chasing my dreams. I am still working on my purpose. I still want to thrive, not just survive.

Some days, I will get everything right.

Some days, I will stumble.

Some days, I will have no idea what I'm doing.

But I will keep going. Because this is my life, and I refuse to let fear run the show.

To anyone reading this who feels like they're stuck in an endless cycle of anxiety—please know this: You are not alone. You don't need anybody but just yourself. You are not weak. And you are absolutely capable of building a life that feels *good*.

Start small.

Be kind to yourself.

Keep moving forward.

You don't have to have it all figured out to start thriving. You just have to believe that you can. And trust me—you *can*.

12 Whole Food Plant-Based Recipes for Anxiety Relief

Anxiety can be overwhelming, but the right foods can help. A whole-food, plant-based diet is rich in nutrients that support brain health, balance hormones, and keep blood sugar levels stable—all essential for managing anxiety.

I've carefully selected these recipes based on my own experiences with food and stress. Each one is not only easy to make but also packed with ingredients known for their calming effects. Whether it's magnesium-rich greens, omega-3-packed seeds, gut-friendly fiber, or mood-boosting fruits, every bite is designed to nourish both body and mind.

Smoothies

1. Calming Green Mango Smoothie

Servings: 2

Why This Recipe?

I've always found that mango brings an instant mood lift. Pairing it with greens makes it a power-packed smoothie for an anxious mind. Spinach provides magnesium, which relaxes the nervous system, and mango gives a serotonin boost.

Ingredients

- o 1 ripe mango, peeled and chopped
- o 1 cup baby spinach
- o 1 small banana
- o 1 cup coconut water
- o Juice of ½ lime

Method

- o Blend all the ingredients until smooth.
- o Serve chilled.

Variations

- o Swap mango with pineapple for a tropical twist.
- o Add a small piece of fresh ginger for a digestion-friendly boost.

Tip

Drink this on an empty stomach in the morning for the best absorption of nutrients.

2. Banana & Dates Anxiety-Relief Smoothie

Servings: 2

Why This Recipe?

Bananas and dates are both natural serotonin boosters, making them perfect for an anxiety-easing drink. Plus, this smoothie is naturally sweet and incredibly filling.

Ingredients

- o 1 ripe banana
- o 2 Medjool dates (pitted)
- o 1 cup coconut water
- o ½ teaspoon cinnamon
- o 1 cup ice

Method

- o Blend all ingredients until smooth.
- o Serve immediately.

Tip

For extra creaminess, freeze the banana before blending.

Breakfast

3. Ragi & Jaggery Porridge

Servings: 2

Why This Recipe?

Ragi is rich in calcium and amino acids that help relax the mind. I love starting my day with this warm, comforting porridge—it's like a hug in a bowl.

Ingredients

- o   ¼ cup ragi flour

- o   1 ½ cups water

- o   1 tbsp jaggery

- o   ½ tsp cardamom powder

- o   1 tbsp chopped nuts (optional)

Method

- o   Mix ragi flour with ½ cup water to make a smooth paste.

- o   Boil the remaining water, add the paste, and stir continuously.

- o   Add jaggery and cardamom, mix well, and cook until thickened.

- o   Serve warm.

Tip

Add grated coconut for extra flavor.

4. Chia & Sabja Seed Pudding

Servings: 2

Why This Recipe?

Chia and sabja seeds are packed with omega-3s, essential for brain health and anxiety relief. This pudding keeps me full and energized throughout the morning.

Ingredients

- o   2 tbsp chia seeds
- o   1 tbsp sabja seeds
- o   1 cup almond milk
- o   1 tbsp date paste
- o   ½ tsp cinnamon
- o   ½ banana, sliced

Method

- o   Soak chia and sabja seeds in almond milk overnight.
- o   Stir in date paste and cinnamon before serving.
- o   Top with banana slices.

Tip

For a twist, add cocoa powder for a chocolate flavor.

Meal Replacement Salad

5. Millet & Chickpea Salad

Servings: 2

Why This Recipe?

Millets are rich in tryptophan, which promotes serotonin production. Chickpeas add protein, making this salad a wholesome meal.

Ingredients

- o   1 cup cooked millet
- o   ½ cup boiled chickpeas
- o   1 cucumber, diced
- o   1 tomato, diced
- o   Juice of 1 lemon
- o   1 tsp cumin powder
- o   Pink salt to taste

Method

- o   Toss all ingredients together.
- o   Let it sit for 10 minutes before serving.

6. High-Protein Tofu & Sprouts Salad

Servings: 2

Why This Recipe?

This is my go-to salad when I need something **light yet filling**. Sprouts and tofu provide protein, which helps stabilize mood, while lemon and coriander make it refreshing.

Ingredients

- o   1 cup mixed sprouts (moong, chana, or masoor)
- o   ½ cup tofu, cubed and lightly pan-seared
- o   ½ cucumber, chopped

- o   ½ onion, finely chopped
- o   1 small carrot, grated
- o   ½ tsp roasted cumin powder
- o   Juice of 1 lemon
- o   1 tbsp chopped coriander
- o   Pink salt to taste

Method

- o   Mix all ingredients in a bowl.
- o   Toss well and let it sit for 10 minutes before eating.

Tip

Add some pomegranate seeds for a burst of sweetness.

7. Sweet Potato & Spinach Chaat Salad

Servings: 2

Why This Recipe?

Sweet potatoes are rich in complex carbs that **keep blood sugar stable**, reducing anxiety. Spinach is loaded with magnesium, known to **calm the nervous system**.

Ingredients

- o   1 medium sweet potato, boiled and cubed
- o   1 cup baby spinach, chopped
- o   1 small cucumber, diced

- o   1 small tomato, chopped
- o   ½ tsp chaat masala
- o   ½ tsp cumin powder
- o   Juice of ½ lemon
- o   1 tbsp chopped mint leaves

Method

- o   Combine all ingredients in a bowl.
- o   Toss well and serve.

Tip

For a crunchy texture, sprinkle some roasted peanuts.

Soups

8. Pumpkin & Ginger Soup

Servings: 2

Why This Recipe?

Pumpkin is rich in **tryptophan, which converts into serotonin**, the happy hormone. Ginger soothes digestion, which is often disturbed by anxiety.

Ingredients

- o   1 cup pumpkin, diced
- o   ½ inch ginger, grated
- o   2 cups water
- o   ½ tsp turmeric
- o   Salt & pepper to taste

Method

- o   Boil pumpkin and ginger in water until soft.
- o   Blend into a smooth soup and season with turmeric, salt, and pepper.

Tip

Add a dash of coconut milk for extra creaminess.

9. Drumstick & Moringa Soup

Servings: 2

Why This Recipe?

Drumsticks and moringa are **rich in iron and antioxidants**, reducing stress and fatigue. This is an immunity-boosting soup, perfect for days when stress makes you feel exhausted.

Ingredients

- o   2 drumsticks, cut into pieces
- o   1 tsp moringa powder (or fresh moringa leaves)
- o   1 small tomato, chopped
- o   2 cups water
- o   ½ tsp black pepper
- o   Salt to taste

Method

- o Boil drumsticks and tomatoes in water.

- o Mash the drumsticks to extract pulp and strain the soup.

- o Stir in moringa powder and season with salt and pepper.

Tip

Enjoy warm before bedtime to **relax and sleep better**.

Desserts (With Cacao)

5. Anxiety-Relief Chocolate Banana Pudding

Servings: 2

Why This Recipe?

Dark cacao **boosts serotonin** levels, which help ease anxiety. This dessert is **guilt-free, naturally sweetened, and takes just 5 minutes** to make!

Ingredients

- o 2 ripe bananas

- o 1 tbsp cacao powder

- o 1 tbsp date paste

- o ½ tsp cinnamon

- o ½ tsp vanilla extract (optional)

Method

- o   Blend all ingredients until smooth.

- o   Refrigerate for 10 minutes before serving.

Tip

Top with grated coconut for extra texture.

6. No-Bake Chocolate Almond Squares

Servings: 8 squares

Why This Recipe?

When I crave chocolate but don't want refined sugar, these cacao squares **save the day**! The combination of cacao, almonds, and dates **boosts energy** and keeps anxiety in check.

Ingredients

- o   1 cup almonds

- o   1 cup dates, pitted

- o   2 tbsp cacao powder

- o   ½ tsp cinnamon

- o   1 tbsp coconut flour

Method

- o   Blend almonds into a coarse meal.

- o   Add dates, cacao powder, and cinnamon, and blend again.

o   Press the mixture into a tray and refrigerate for 1 hour.

o   Cut into squares and enjoy.

Tip

Sprinkle a pinch of sea salt to enhance the chocolate flavor.

Snacks

7. Spiced Roasted Chickpeas

Servings: 2

Why This Recipe?

Chickpeas are **rich in protein and fiber**, preventing mood crashes. This snack is crispy, crunchy, and **perfect for stress eating** (in a healthy way!).

Ingredients

o   1 cup boiled chickpeas

o   ½ tsp turmeric

o   ½ tsp cumin powder

o   ½ tsp chili powder

o   Salt to taste

Method

- o Toss chickpeas with spices and dry roast for 10 minutes.

- o Serve warm or store in an airtight container.

Tip

Use an air fryer for a crispier texture.

8. Date & Coconut Laddoos

Servings: 6 laddoos

Why This Recipe?

Dates provide natural sweetness and are **rich in B vitamins**, essential for **nervous system health**.

Ingredients

- o 1 cup dates, pitted

- o ½ cup grated coconut

- o ½ tsp cardamom powder

Method

- o Blend all ingredients into a dough-like consistency.

- o Roll into small laddoos and refrigerate for 30 minutes before serving.

Tip

Coat with sesame seeds for extra crunch.

Final Thoughts

These **meal replacement salads, soups, cacao-based desserts, and snacks** are easy to make, rich in **stress-busting nutrients**, and perfect for **managing anxiety naturally**.

Food has been a huge part of my **healing journey**. When I eat foods that support my nervous system, I feel **calmer, more focused, and less reactive**.

Try these recipes, experiment with flavors, and **find what makes you feel your best!**